BEYOND

A LIVING PERSON'S GUIDE TO THE DEAD

TIFFANY HOPKINS

STERLING ETHOS
New York

STERLING ETHOS
New York

STERLING ETHOS and the distinctive Sterling Ethos logo
are registered trademarks of Sterling Publishing Co., Inc.

Text © 2025 Tiffany Hopkins

All rights reserved. No part of this publication may be reproduced,
stored in a retrieval system, or transmitted in any form or by any means
(including electronic, mechanical, photocopying, recording, or otherwise)
without prior written permission from the publisher.

ISBN 978-1-4549-5839-0
ISBN 978-1-4549-5840-6 (e-book)

Library of Congress Control Number: 2024951761

For information about custom editions,
special sales, and premium purchases, please
contact specialsales@unionsquareandco.com.

Printed in the United States of America

2 4 6 8 10 9 7 5 3 1

unionsquareandco.com

Cover design by Pete Garceau
Cover image by panimoni/iStock/Getty Images Plus (gradient)
Interior design by Christine Heun

Dedicated to all the mediums, past, present,
and future. Because a lot is said regarding mediumship,
and ne'er a word about it being easy.

CONTENTS

Introduction viii

PART I. **CHOOSING MEDIUMSHIP** 1
CHAPTER 1. **MEDIUMSHIP IS FOR EVERYONE, JUST NOT ME** 3
CHAPTER 2. **CONCEPTUAL FRAMEWORKS** 11
CHAPTER 3. **BEING A RESPONSIBLE MEDIUM** 40

PART II. **THE REASON(S) FOR MEDIUMSHIP** 72
CHAPTER 4. **NOT QUITE BORN AGAIN** 74
CHAPTER 5. **HEALING THROUGH CONNECTION** 87
CHAPTER 6. **IMAGINATION AS EXPLORATION** 116
CHAPTER 7. **MEDIUMSHIP FOR MONEY** 133

PART III. **GIVING RISE TO MEDIUMSHIP** 140
CHAPTER 8. **FORMING METHODS** 142
CHAPTER 9. **MEDIUMSHIP FOR CREATIVITY** 160
CHAPTER 10. **DEVELOPMENT CIRCLES** 176
CHAPTER 11. **OFFERING READINGS** 200

Conclusion 219
Notes 222
Resources 225
Index 238
Acknowledgments 244
About the Author 246

INTRODUCTION

Introducing people to *mediumship* usually requires a long preamble to reassure the listener that I have not fallen off the deep end, or at least that I am knowingly swimming there. A few places in the world, hiding in plain sight, do not require such a song and dance. Some are right here in the United States—tiny communities of Spiritualists, a religion that centers around communication with the dead. In a surprise move at age thirty-four, I settled in one, and this has been the place where I learned to be a *medium*.

If someone is here, they are presumed to believe that talking to the dead is possible. With that out of the way, conversations open up quickly. If you remain here, learning unfolds in a little cocoon, and you can forget that the rest of the world still needs that preamble.

Once I recognized this gift a like-minded community had made for me, I wanted to extend the cocoon. I made a website, Normalize Talking to the Dead (NT2TD), weaving together research, media, and resources for my fellow mediums. This book is one such resource intended for anyone curious about mediumship. You will find a lot of preamble; whole sections of the book are dedicated to whether or not one should, can, and may practice mediumship, as well as why one might want to, before we get to the how. Mediumship is a capacity that every human has, so the baseline skill is turning it on and off. To get there, however, we might need to reorganize what we think is and is not possible. Then, we manage the consequences of doing something our society considers taboo. All this is best done with others—and there are plenty of us doing this work. You don't have to go it alone.

Introduction

The preamble, philosophy, history, research, and storytelling in this book are meant to provide as many inroads to mediumship as possible. Cultural expectations may give you a certain idea of who a medium is and what they do—throw that away. Everyone can integrate mediumship into their lives in whatever way suits them. As a tool for relating with the unseen, mediumship helps us forge connections when we don't have all the information we need. Whether during work hours, on the road far from home, in the depths of an intimate relationship, or while reflecting on one's own, we can all relate to wishing we could better understand each other. Mediumship is usually associated with talking to the dead, but I hope to show that it is a skill that can be used in any atypical communication setting—from pets to plants to planets to parts of the body.

I invite my readers to visit Spiritualist communities and feel the cocoon in real life. Even better, make your own community where talking to the dead is normal. I hope some of my readers will become professional mediums. Just as much, I want to support the educators, creatives, parents, managers, care workers, and everyone else who will go on to use mediumship in their everyday lives. For those who hire mediums, you will be better prepared to choose the right person and make the most of your session. This book will take you outside the confines of religion—and spirituality—to find ways to bring this skill back into the world with art, community, nature, activism, healing, and all the other worthy human tasks involving *connection*.

To go beyond, we must start within. The modern world doesn't offer a helpful context for being fully present in our being, nor for developing and using mediumship. Normalizing talking to the dead will take some time for the outside world—but we have the capacity to make change within ourselves at any moment. Throughout this book, I will invite you to connect directly with the unseen, unheard, unfelt, unsmelled, untasted, and unknown world around us. To support your travel beyond the page, I've included exercises and guided meditations. Many

Introduction

chapters also include questions to journal, think through, or discuss. At the end of the book are notes and resources for each chapter, offering many more places to expand your learning. Visit normalizetalkingtothedead.com for a glossary of all the key terms in the book, a directory of practitioners, other extras, and to join the community. See you on the other side!

PART I

CHOOSING MEDIUMSHIP

What do you think of when you hear the word *mediumship*? Give yourself a moment to allow images, words, feelings, and memories to emerge.

What about only the word *medium*? Again, stop and think for a moment. What comes up? T-shirts, tempera paint, tech media companies? The word serves the same purpose in each case: a medium is in between—between humans and *spirits*, between small and large, between an artist and their expression. When we become mediums, we hold together two states: we connect.

This is a book about talking to the dead. But why limit ourselves to talking when we have so many ways to connect? Verbal expression, body and facial language, gestures and movement, attention, feeling and empathy, listening and questioning, storytelling, music, art, symbology—all that makes us richly communicative beings. Mediumship is the application of communication skills we already have to a new context: it asks us to connect the living with the dead temporarily. This is a challenge because the dead have no matter with which to engage—they do not exist in our material world. We must find ways to connect with their nonphysical selves from our physical form.

If we can build this bridge between the living and dead, why not try it in some of the other contexts where we struggle with communication? Many more potential *contacts* are nonphysical or unreliably physical, such as fictional characters, our future or past selves, collective consciousness, deities and other cultural figures, and other dimensions. There are also plenty of options in the physical world, where the distinction between living and nonliving is less of a hurdle than profoundly different methods of communication. These potential contacts include people who speak other languages or not at all, plants, animals, minerals, our bodies, art and other objects, Earth, and space.

This definition of *mediumship* includes but pushes past talking to the dead. It is a nonmaterial or spiritual tool for connection. A *medium* is someone who uses this tool to experience connection that extends the bounds of their material form.

Rather than continuing to use the negative case, *non-*, which denotes a "lack of," *meta-*, which implies "above," or *extra-*, which means "outside," to define our areas of interest, we'll use the Latin prefix *trans-*. *Trans* means "beyond," such as the *transphysical* world (which is beyond the physical world), *transliving* (those who are beyond life in bodily form), and *transordinary* (beyond our usual reality, as compared with extraordinary, which is outside the ordinary). With this language, we open up the space to move into the transordinary, starting from within our reality and maintaining our connection to it wherever we go.

CHAPTER 1

MEDIUMSHIP IS FOR EVERYONE, JUST NOT ME

The drive from Brooklyn to Lily Dale took twelve hours through mile upon mile of snowstorm. When we finally made it, four feet of fluffy powder had accumulated. On New Year's Day, 2018, I pulled up to the cottage in my U-Haul truck with Nika the Dog in the passenger seat. Behind me, my sister Hannah followed in an SUV filled with all my (soon-to-be-frozen) plants. My uncle Gary had told me the cottage was uninhabitable after twenty years of neglect, but I assumed he thought I was a city slicker and was overstating things. As it turned out, the place *was* uninhabitable.

We got out and looked around, trudging through the snow in duct-taped boots and borrowed coveralls. Right away we saw there was no water, and no wood for the woodstove, the only source of heat. All we had inherited was twenty years of dust, multiple truckloads' worth of trash, five generations of broken furniture, miscellaneous supplies from past repair attempts, and two dead birds that had been there so long only the bones remained. But still, I knew I would stay.

My first order of business was to meet my neighbors. And, being a "when in Rome" person, I found my way to a community mediumship class as soon as the storm let up. I knew this town was involved with mediumship, but I didn't know exactly what that meant, at least initially. I learned quickly that Lily Dale is the world's largest community of Spiritualists, in the tradition of the Modern

American Spiritualism movement. Since the 1870s, thousands of people have gathered here each year to talk to the dead with the help of the residents, many of whom work as professional mediums.

Throughout my life, logic has been extremely important to me. I developed my intellect for many reasons, including not wanting to appear foolish, unreliable, or different. I relied personally and professionally on numbers, mathematics, the harder sciences, and data to counteract these fears. Mediumship put me back in direct contact with them. It asked me to do something that most people consider incredibly foolish: speak with—and for—the dead. It is notoriously unreliable. And it is most definitely not normal.

Defining mediumship is complicated, but I quickly realized after moving to Lily Dale that there are no limitations on who can participate. Anyone can become a medium. However, I didn't intend to become one myself. Nobody has been more surprised than me that this is what I spend my free time doing. I came to Lily Dale to avoid paying rent, to give my dog a place to run, and to see if I could get healthy and happy away from the city.

That anyone can be a medium is the foundational principle of Modern American Spiritualism, a socio-spiritual—and later, religious—movement that emerged from western New York during a nineteenth-century American revival called the Second Great Awakening. This movement reacquainted many people in the United States with the idea that anyone can practice mediumship to prove that the soul's existence does not end with death.

Almost 200 years later, I became one of those people. Although the cottage has been in the family for five generations, it came to me through not a biological relative but my bonus dad, whom my mom married when I was four. I was not looking to talk to the dead and was surprised to find in mediumship the connection to myself I'd struggled to establish in my life.

Being an adult often means turning toward what feels certain: establishing a home, finding a job, making money. I was no different—I built a career in tech innovation that introduced me to brilliant people and helped me feel financially stable. I enjoyed a modern life of wonder and excitement. In the process, I gave up making music and art; performing in theater, sports, and dance, and my voracious appetite for reading. In my early life, those interests propelled me, as I was consumed by boundless energy and an intense drive to learn more. But the older I got, the less I entertained them.

In my twenties, I went to business school. I chose a dual degree program in Switzerland (for the financial roots) and Singapore (for the focus on technology). By this time, I wasn't thinking at all about creative work. I lived in Europe and Asia, moved to Africa, then spent a season living out of two carry-on suitcases, traipsing across Brazil, Germany, and Australia, showing e-commerce start-ups how to measure their marketing efficiency on the expense account of a venture capital firm.

By this point, my energy was starting to wane. Insensitive bosses and toxic work environments made me question my capacity to subvert my desires for a paycheck. Years of heavy drinking, erratic sleep, and lack of exercise led to odd health issues popping up one after another. Moving from place to place and country to country left me lonely and isolated. I felt powerless in my world and my body.

A few days before my twenty-eighth birthday, sitting in a high-rise in São Paulo, I got a call from my father. He told me that my grandmother, Maxine, to whom I had been very close, had died. I couldn't get back in time to attend the funeral, and that was the final straw. I quit my job and went home. When I landed back in the United States—specifically, in the driver's seat of an '07 Chevy Aveo with my two carry-on suitcases, Rachel Pollack's *Seventy-Eight Degrees of Wisdom*, and a modest collection of gray power suits—I drove around the country looking for somewhere I could put down my roots—or at least a stable place for my things so I could head out on another adventure when the opportunity arose.

After a few months, I found myself with a red, chicken-hunting husky named Nika, whom I rescued from doggy death row. I rented a large house in

East Oakland, California, with my sisters Hannah and Amara and three other roommates. I tried to start a consulting practice, studied Earth-based wisdom, and relearned how to care for myself. My teacher at the time was Marza Millar, a medical intuitive, herbalist, healer, and medicine woman with whom I still work. It took a few false starts there, in Nevada City, California, and Brooklyn, New York, before this new approach to life became apparent. I had been missing so much connection: with my body, with *creativity*, with animals and nature, with community.

That was my state of mind when I heard about a house my uncle Gary inherited but didn't want—that dilapidated cottage in Lily Dale. I saw that house as my way to free myself from a life that required me to disconnect from the essential things. I could be near my last remaining grandparent, in the place where family had lived for generations. I could reacquaint myself with my roots since I had grown up in the area before moving west with my family when I was eight. And finally, I hoped that by living in this rural location, I could reduce my expenditure enough to work through the lean years of building my business, an innovation and modernization consulting practice, which I hoped would give me financial independence.

I have been able to do these things. And in the process, I also fell in love with talking to the dead. The skills I have learned have helped me find freedom. At its core, mediumship is an act of relating within the internal experience. It asked me to slowly and consciously develop my *imagination*, capacity for *presence*, connection to my body's intuition, and awareness of and responsibility for my mind. It asked me to join a community and build a digital outgrowth expanding beyond a rural hamlet in western New York. It also allowed me to dive deep, explore what it means to be a medium, and develop a few ideas about how it works.

Mediumship Is for Everyone, Just Not Me

This book began as a research paper for a two-year prophecy and spiritual healing program at Fellowships of the Spirit, an independent Spiritualist church and school right outside the gates of Lily Dale, which I joined less than a year after I arrived. At the time, I was curious about *channeling* or receiving information from transphysical sources for creative purposes. I experimented, researched, and wrote about it for the graduation requirement. I found a dozen writers and spiritual folks who explained how to channel, but I was crestfallen each time I read their suggestions, which can be summarized as:

1. Get a pencil or pen.
2. Connect to spirit.
3. Write.

This kicked my rational, framework-loving, data-driven brain into gear. There had to be more to it than that. So, I did what I always do when trying to figure something out: I made a spreadsheet. Each time I practiced channeling, I entered it into my little database.

DATE	TIME	LENGTH	INTENTION	OUTPUT	PROCESS	FORMAT
9/14/19	12:58 p.m.	16 mins	Connect with guide who can share wisdom on focus	Instagram post	None	Typed
9/23/19	3:19 p.m.	20 mins	Where to begin my research on channeling?	Instagram post	Breathing	Typed
9/26/19	7:13 p.m.	15 mins	Josefa's mediumship session	Pages 7 and 8 of Chapter 12	Meditation	Typed
10/30/19	3:39 p.m.	7 mins	Exercise	Single page	DailyOM	Typed
11/12/19	6:52 p.m.	19 mins	What should I call the podcast?	Podcast name	S. Brown	Written
12/28/19	9:08 p.m.	22 mins	How should I focus my efforts?	Work plan	M. Young	Written
3/23/20	9:40 a.m.	18 mins	What healing is best for the service?	Healing service	J. Rochester	Typed
4/13/20	1:23 p.m.	8 mins	Clarity on the purpose of this paper	Outline	None	Written

A sample of my early "spirit writing sessions" data. Find references for the processes at the end of the book.

I found that even with a relatively weak connection to some unidentified "spirit," I enjoyed the process and produced results more easily than by simply thinking. I wanted to make this repeatable, a method I could rely upon when confronted with unknowns.

As I started parsing out the steps, I recognized what happened as a form of the typical, client-based mediumship and spiritual healing I was learning at Fellowships. The first version of my "methodology" was a mashup of what I did when I interviewed someone for a research project, what I did when I talked to the dead, and how I experienced healing energy in the body:

1. Gathering materials
2. Focusing
3. Relaxing the mind and body
4. Connecting
5. Writing
6. Closing the connection

I also perceived mediumship as potentially beneficial to everyone I know. I felt the threads of more than only creativity helping me weave new ways to talk about this elusive, muddy, uncouth practice. Everything I did became a new way to look at mediumship: mindfulness, somatics, experimentation, innovation, psychology, ecology, community development, software development, cognitive science, social justice. Enshrining the tools for reaching outside my mind in spirituality meant depriving most of my friends, family members, and colleagues of an essential part of the human experience I wanted to share with them. So I set about uncovering it.

My career transversed continents, sectors, and every type of organization. Time and again I've served as a bridge between groups. I've been the most creative person in a technical room and the most technical person in a creative room.

Sometimes I'm the most business-minded person in a room of free spirits or the most free-spirited in a room of businesspeople. I am somehow both a skeptic in a room of mediums and a mediumship evangelist in a room of skeptics. I realized that, with this ability to sit between communities, I could tell other people how I did what I did and how they could do it, too.

Although it has been fewer than seven years since I sat in my first mediumship class, I have spent a remarkable amount of time talking, studying, experimenting, and writing in excruciating detail on the subject by taking it out of its usual context. It is still mysterious, but it is also right here waiting for you.

Much of this book may not appear to be about mediumship at first glance. I've gathered the components of my experience that most clearly contribute to my practice. You don't need a special gift, specific objects, or certain beliefs to practice most of what you'll read in this book—just curiosity, care for yourself and others, and a willingness to navigate ambiguity.

As part of my research, I developed a survey and sent it to my network of mediums, *psychics*, healers, artists, animal communicators, and other types of practitioners. It is a representative survey of my community, not of the wider industry or practitioners in general. The forty-one respondents are very experienced, with 40 percent practicing for over twenty-five years. Seventy-five percent work in an official or professional capacity, and 44 percent are people I met in Lily Dale. (Find a directory of these practitioners on https://www.normalizetalkingtothedead.com/directory.)

The last question on the survey asked what respondents wished someone had told them earlier in their development. They said mediumship development is more than the "hard skills" like psychic abilities, energetic hygiene, and protection. They wished they'd had a supportive environment that promoted normalization and acceptance of these practices. They said a community could have helped them build confidence for personal growth and practical skills for

Beyond

integrating mediumship into their daily lives. That could have helped them experiment, overcome skepticism and misconceptions, and learn continuously in a supportive environment. I hope this book enables us to build such a community so that we can all continue developing our abilities.

---

1. Take a few moments to consider what would need to happen for you to call yourself a medium or, if you already do, what happened to bring you to that conclusion.

2. What do you think society considers a medium? Do you subscribe to those definitions?

3. What has been your mediumship journey so far? Allow your imagination to take you into the future. What do you hope you learn, experience, and try?

CHAPTER 2

CONCEPTUAL FRAMEWORKS

The first time I was asked, "Are you a medium?" was at the dentist's office. I was surprised and looked around, which accurately indicated to the inquirer I didn't understand why she was asking. She said she had looked at my chart and saw my address. That day I learned that people in the region usually know of Lily Dale and what it's about. It felt like such a complicated question to me. I started to explain, rambling the complicated answer, "Yes, I am learning, I'm in a two-year program and I practice as a student but I am not registered in Lily Dale . . ." She wasn't listening anymore. I realized that some people aren't asking philosophical, moral, or technical questions. They want to know if you'll give them a reading.

Not long after, returning from Canada near Buffalo, the border patrolman asked me the same thing when I told him where I lived. As I stammered out my awkward, unsure response, I realized how suspicious I sounded. He kept asking me questions about being a medium and what was required to live in Lily Dale as I nervously looked in my rearview mirror to see if a line was forming. Several very long minutes later, he handed back my passport. The questioning had nothing to do with the border—he had visited Lily Dale as a kid and (mis)remembered that everyone who lived there was required to be a medium.

Becoming a medium is like being an artist or activist: a constellation of skills, mindsets, and experiences that become part of a person's life. From the outside, these things may look binary—I am or I am not. Rarely is it so simple.

Is a particular milestone or capacity the bar for acceptance? One of the beauties and complexities of our current time is that we recognize that nothing is black and white. You get to decide if and when you become a medium.

In the spring of 2023, Pew Research found that 53 percent of American adults say they've been "visited by a dead family member in a dream or some other form" during their lives. *More than half of us.* That doesn't mean everyone believes in mediumship, but it does make more than half of us mediums.

If you come to this book questioning whether mediumship is genuine, that's okay. Entertain the idea that anyone who desires can be a medium. If this is true, you are the best person to answer whether mediumship is genuine. Try out the tools, and base your determination on personal experience.

We need two things to become a medium: faith and proof. Each person needs their own levels of each. At some points, we need faith. It enables us to jump into the unknown. At other junctures, we require proof. We must turn around and head back to stable ground. They are the chicken and the egg. Some of us are egg people; we need proof first. Some of us are chicken people; we start with faith. Regardless of what starts us on our path, we need both to keep going. We earn our faith and our proof through action. We accumulate experiences that help us to know whether to jump or turn back.

As science turns molecules into atoms and particles into quarks, a nagging question remains: Is there anything "real" that cannot be measured? Can something truly exist if it only occurs in our interior experience? What if that experience is limited to a single individual, not replicable or even shareable? It is a relief to rely on the measurable, in black and white for all to see. This need for certainty and focus on the tangible world has developed at pace with our ability to measure an increasingly broad spectrum of phenomena at an increasingly wide scope.

Mediumship, like our feelings, dreams, ideas, and memories, is an intangible element of life that can challenge our concept of what is and is not "real." I'd love to wave it all off and relegate it to semantics. *Real*, *love*, and *feeling* are all insufficient—we need new words. As a language uniquely comfortable with borrowing, I'm certain that English will expand to fit the bill. But we have a bigger challenge: changing our thinking, acting, and being.

In the past few hundred years, we have gone from relying purely on religion to explain reality to an odd hodgepodge of religion and science. Science has benefits—we cannot return to bloodletting and unalterable rules from a two-thousand-year-old book. But by the same token, we cannot relinquish our internal worlds and every shred of mystery. Religion and science have created a doorway of understanding for us, with faith holding up one side and reason holding up the other.

We now must decide if we can handle walking through that door and accept that both are real and have limitations. It may be time for a secret third thing to take hold, and this already happens every day through our experiences. In them, we are offered a reality where some things are material and some are spiritual. There is overlap. To recognize everything in this reality, we may have to concede that there are some things we cannot know.

I have struggled with this mindset for most of my life, and my unknowing has only been amplified by my work with mediumship. I'm happy to offer you this sacred and liberatory struggle, too. Welcome, my friend. Let us walk this winding and sometimes invisible road together.

To give you a way to form your own opinions on mediumship, I will start with a few current and past explanations I've come across. Some are more compatible with this book than others, but I have taken pains so that most people can go beyond without accepting my beliefs.

At the same time, I ask that now and throughout the book you consider what it would take to change your mind—from wherever you find yourself. Every time you arrive at a new understanding, enjoy the certainty for a moment. Just don't let it rest for too long before you again look for what it would take to go beyond.

In his book *Death as an Altered State of Consciousness*, consciousness researcher and psychology professor Imants Barušs uses the term *boggle threshold*, or "degree to which a person is willing to deviate from normative beliefs." To understand what could be considered normative, I will place various explanations of mediumship on a spectrum from materialist (relating to matter) to spiritualist (not relating to matter). Materialist approaches focus on whether mediumship is possible and, if so, through what mechanism. Spiritualist approaches tend to believe they can happen (especially in this book's broader definition of mediumship), focusing on who may engage in the practice on both sides of the connection.

Although far from an exhaustive overview, these are the most common positions I've come across, and most readers will be familiar with at least some of them. All may be considered elements of our current cultural viewpoint of mediumship, potentially influencing our beliefs.

Materialist Approaches

Materialism posits that existence is bound by what is materially present. The purest materialist approach would deem none of the topics in this book possible. However, neuroscience has shown that humans receive, process, and act upon information with conscious awareness *and* at the unconscious level. For example, the physiological process of *neuroception* is the mechanism by which the nervous system "reads" the environment and people around us to determine safety and produce the appropriate neurological state. Humans are constantly interpreting extremely complex situations without knowing the full extent of where we're getting our information.

While presumed to be sensory input, we do not yet know on what scale this is happening or if transphysical data is included in our processing. This could be as simple as when a medium gives another person (we'll refer to the recipient of mediumship as a *sitter*) a message from the dead—they could pick up on the unconscious actions of the sitter and interpret them as information coming from the dead.

Conceptual Frameworks

Mentalists openly explain that they provide their readings and *séances* using repeatable mechanisms based on reading body language ("tricks") and researching participants ahead of time ("hot" readings). People tend to enjoy mentalist performances despite knowing they are not "real," but tricks and hot readings are considered fraudulent mediumship.

Another theory is that instead of picking up on subtle nonverbal cues from the sitter, the medium uses their subconscious material as content for messages. This could include snap judgments and information based on biases, a known issue for all interpersonal relationships that is avoidable, to some extent, with time and effort. Again, the problem arises if the medium does not disclose or acknowledge this.

One step away from materialism is to include the possibility of psychic communication or extrasensory perception (ESP) to enable *transphysical communication* (TPC). This still sits on the spectrum of explanations encompassing the natural human ability to receive, process, and act upon information of which they may or may not be aware. This theory does not require believing in the potential to access individuals after death. By suggesting that information about the dead comes from the sitter, TPC also offers one plausible answer for those who believe in reincarnation or otherwise that an individual does not remain as such after death.

TPC involves the medium picking up on any number of invisible (in other words, not currently measurable and therefore not acknowledged by science) data sources from their sitter. This could allow the medium to access the sitter's memories, thoughts, internal physiology, and emotions. Two ways this has been theorized are through energy given off by the sitter or the medium's ability to access the sitter's internal experience directly.

In addition to a general concept of "energy," the microscopic beings within us, as well as DNA, could be sources of information. Our hearts beat and exude a measurable energy. Only half of each of us are human cells—the rest of our bodies are made up of water, minerals, air, and trillions of microbes, all living their lives in our bodies, each making and using tiny amounts of energy. Less than 10 percent of our DNA is uniquely human, meaning we share building blocks with other living beings and extinct hominid species. Perhaps, with very finely tuned senses, we can pick up on the memory of a deceased loved one from DNA.

Psychic capacities have been explored by the studies of parapsychology labs in dozens of countries and in the United States at major universities (the most famous at Duke, but others at Stanford, Princeton, and University of California, Los Angeles), government agencies (many funded by the Central Intelligence Agency), and independent organizations (like the Rhine Research Center and Institute of Noetic Sciences). There are also individuals who have conducted conclusive studies on animal communication, such as Dr. Rupert Sheldrake, and telepathy savants, like Dr. Diane Hennacy Powell.

One independent organization, the Windbridge Research Center, has conducted several recent studies on mediumship that hold up to a few different scientific standards. One study showed that 81 percent of the time, a person could identify between a *mediumship reading* for themselves and one for another person. This study was triple blinded, a form of experimental design where the parties involved are unaware of certain aspects of the study to prevent bias. Triple blinding provides a high level of scientific rigor, making it a gold standard in experimental research. It was also peer-reviewed five times and published in two different scientific journals. A meta-analysis of studies on mediums' accuracy found that "some mediums are able to acquire information about deceased persons through some unknown or anomalous means."

Many who have experienced ESP maintain that their capacity for the phenomenon is accessed through heightened emotions, making laboratory tasks a poor test. They are devoid of real-world connection and therefore any emotional charge. This could speak to how a medium would be able to pick up on the exact thing the sitter hopes to discuss, given that the subject holds ample emotional or energetic space for them.

One step further into the unknown is a rather elegant solution positing that a medium can (whether they know it or not) travel to the past to see the sitter's loved ones alive or into the future to see what kinds of things might happen for them, then bring that information back as a message.

Finally, quantum theory offers another way to look at psychic and mediumistic phenomena. The simplest possibility, although not the only way to look at it, is that behavior observed at the quantum level could be possible at the *consciousness* level. In other words, we could have the capacity to exist as a point (an individual) or a wave (connected through time and space to ourselves or others). The philosophical and scientific frontiers of consciousness are constantly changing. One way I have kept up with the latest is through Jeffrey Kripal's work. His 2019 book, *The Flip*, is a good place to start.

Spiritualist Approaches

On the other side is faith-based understandings of mediumship that mainly occur within religion. This is likely where many of us first encounter the concept. In the most general sense, nearly all religions are spiritualist, as they value life's nonmaterial (transphysical) aspects. Because of this, long-standing traditions, foundational texts, and established practices often, at some level, exist to prove the ability of humans to be in contact with something more than themselves. They do this in very different ways. Modern American Spiritualism, perhaps one of the most overt examples, uses mediumship to prove the soul's existence after death.

The rest of the world's religions broadly vary regarding what is appropriate to communicate with and who is allowed to develop or participate in the connection. The most general view across the diverse adherents to Abrahamic religions (Islam, Judaism, Christianity) is a highly regulated system where contact is presumed only to happen with God and his messengers by those who have been granted permission to do so through their respective policies. There are several passages in the Bible regarding talking with spirits, including the Holy Spirit. However, communication with the dead is generally frowned upon, if not outright banned, in most mainstream sects. While still rarely permitting association with the dead, esoteric or mystic offshoots (e.g., Sufism, Kabbalah, Gnosticism) may allow those permitted to become adherents to develop their abilities to connect directly to God within well-defined standards and processes.

This contrasts with most other religions, especially in the polytheistic (e.g., Hindu), Dharmic (e.g., Buddhist), and regional religions with an overarching trend that is more open to their adherents communicating with the beyond, in particular as deity and *ancestor veneration*. Traditions and taboos guard who can be connected with whom, and many focus on specific divine spirits, deities, or *lineages*. Most have clergy, initiates, or otherwise delineated specialists to provide clear connections for the group and others. Regardless, individuals are encouraged, if not expected, to manage their connections at some level and to the best of their abilities.

Mixed Abrahamic and regional religions, such as the African-diaspora religions (a few of the most well-known being voodoo, Santeria, and Rastafarianism), were built slowly over the past few centuries of often forced adoption of Christianity. This created religions that merge certain parts of each tradition, focusing on regular, ritualized contact among humans, spirits, and deities. Modern American Spiritualism would also fit into this category, as a mixture of Protestantism (particularly in the tradition of the Quakers), regional Native American religions, African-diaspora religions, Eastern religions (both Hindu and Buddhist), and emergent philosophies from regional and transatlantic movements (such as mesmerism and Owenism). New Age beliefs, in a general sense, could be considered an evolution of this form of *Spiritualism*, in particular the ability of anyone to connect for themselves. New Age has a focus on channeling and forms of contacts like ascended masters and angels.

FINDING BALANCE

At this point in the text, I want to call out that if you're a very heady person, take a moment to notice your body and heart as you read. Let your feelings guide you to discern when to start and when to stop. Follow that energy! If you are more body centered or feel overwhelmed by the text, take breaks to withdraw from the mind and reconnect with your body and your understanding. Follow that heart!

There has been a revival of ancient European religions, such as paganism, Druidry, and Wicca, harkening to pre-Christian European practices of ancestor veneration and more general work with spirits and deities. These rarely exist in an unbroken line like the African diaspora and regional traditions do. Instead, modern folks have revived them with the help of historical artifacts and anthropological study.

Across history, the continued love for ancestors well past their deaths has been a foundational aspect of human culture. Most humans, at some point in their lineage, were part of a culture that believed in the unseen world. In many currently active regional religions worldwide, people have carried this belief through the ages. And many people now and throughout history, like me, go much further than talking to the dead. Some believe that every living thing, sometimes every natural thing, and other times some or all nonliving artifacts are endowed with a consciousness with which we may interact. I use the term *transliving being* to include these intermediary states as well as death.

Creativity can be included in the spiritual ways of understanding mediumship. Although not exclusively a spiritual practice, art is often attributed to inspiration and the divine. In mediumship, like art-making, we externalize an internal experience that emerges through interaction with something outside ourselves.

I cannot warm to the idea that there is a single answer for all humanity or for all time. The materialist approaches generally lack any "why," and the religious lack the "how." In my exposure to spirituality, the common thread I've cultivated is a consciousness and connectivity across all the material world. With it has come a desire to better explain my experience, for which I turned to science. I hope you read through this unreasonably brief overview to pick and choose what interests you, what makes perfect sense, what dismays you, and where you see potential.

Two New Metaphors for Mediumship

To move away from religion and science and into everyday experience, I offer a couple of new ways to look at mediumship. The first is *data processing*, which has helped me think concretely about what happens when we function as mediums. The second is *improvisation*, which has helped me strengthen the act of mediumship.

Data Processing

My two undergraduate degrees, a bachelor of arts in interdisciplinary computing in the arts and music and a bachelor of science in cognitive science, overlapped in the cutting-edge (at the time) discipline of "human-computer interaction." I distinctly remember feeling my first programming class change my brain by requiring me to think of the world as an input/output machine so I could write code that would tell the computer what I wanted it to do. I took as many computer science classes as possible and for three years worked as a teaching assistant for introductory programming classes for non-computer science majors.

I do not believe mediums (or people) are computers, but simplifying how our brains work and thinking of them as input/output machines can be illuminating. Unlike computers, we can, in some part and with practice, choose from where we collect our data, how we receive it, and how we process it. Even with artificial intelligence, at least for now, computers rely on humans as their source. But for most of us, most of the time, and for most practitioners through the ages, these are automatic things. They all happen in this moment of surrender when we become mediums. It is nearly instantaneous and is invisible to the outside world.

Defining Data

Data are individual units of information. In typical use of the word, data can be quantitative (numerical) or qualitative (descriptive). In mediumship, our raw data include everything happening in our body before our conscious awareness: synapses firing, blood flowing, food digesting, hormones coursing. Raw data is automatically monitored and brought into consciousness to use as the processed data of our sensory experiences, bodily sensations, thoughts, and emotions. These processed data create our decisions, behaviors, and expressions.

Where Data Comes From

A *contact* refers to whatever we connect with during mediumship. We can expand that into a *source* by referring to possibilities that are not individuals or beings. There are two main categories of sources: the material world, tangible and measurable, and the transphysical world, which is only experiential.

Within the physical world, we have everything in the here and now, which includes the potential for beings like extraterrestrials (who may be physical entities from very far away), ESP between physical beings (including communication across vast distances), and time travel (not the kind happening in the imagination, but our physical body moving to another time). Within the transphysical world, we have all the cultural *realms* (spirit realm, heaven), the concept of other dimensions, and our entire internal experience, because nobody can measure or detect it.

Everything on the chart opposite, plus anything you can imagine adding to it, is a potential source. At any given moment in a reading, I may receive data from how a sitter smells, my memories of last week, my awareness of their area code, the feeling of their energy, and the communications of their dead.

It is overly simplistic to think we use a single data source at any given time or that the goal is to use one particular source. This is often the assumption with mediumship, but it isn't realistic or desirable. A world-renowned *trance* medium explained to a class I attended that when we first start *trance mediumship*, the connection is something like 3 percent spirit and 97 percent us. She added that even the best mediums will never have connections that are 100 percent spirit, although the connection does get closer to that percentage with the more experience one has.

Mediumship teaches us to turn down some sources and to turn up others, but we are data-processing beings, and to some extent we use what we have. This is why, in the beginning, it is easier to practice mediumship with strangers—we have less information to cloud our more subtle capacities.

The development task with sources is building relationships to navigate among them. The aim is not to control our sources but to respect them and their existence. We can learn to change our focus, turn down the processes of our inner experience, and step away from our analytical mind with its constant suggestions of memories, ideas, and parallels.

How We Collect Data

For these diagrams, I simplified the process of obtaining data into materialist and spiritualist extremes before introducing my hybrid, transbinary theory. The materialist model states that nothing extrasensory is happening. In this understanding, all information comes from within the medium's mind or sensory information from the environment.

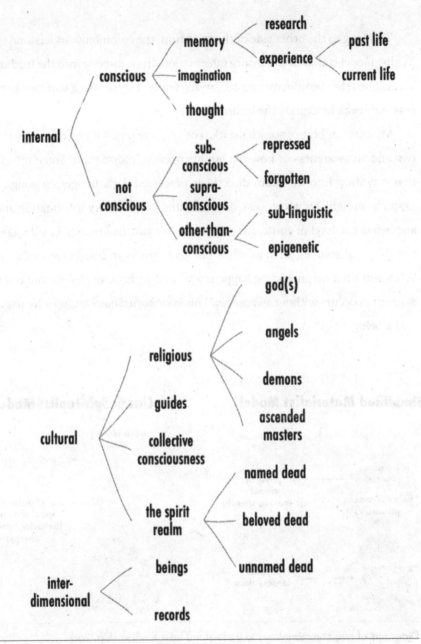

Potential transphsyical sources for data during mediumship. For a chart that includes physical sources and a downloadable version for you to add your own experiences to, visit the NT2TD website.

Beyond

To swing to the other side of the spectrum, the commonly understood spiritualist model is that extrasensory information drops directly into the medium's brain. Then the medium maintains varying levels of conscious awareness to process and speak or express the information.

My current, best conceptualization of all these possibilities combines these two and an awareness of how the body processes information. Some information may drop into the brain directly as processed data, images, or songs, for example, mingling with processed sensory and extrasensory information above and below the level of conscious awareness. We can also receive raw data from transphysical sources, such as when our body reacts to beings we cannot see. While information processing happens with and without awareness, none of the expression occurs without awareness. This is *embodied mediumship*—we use our entire being.

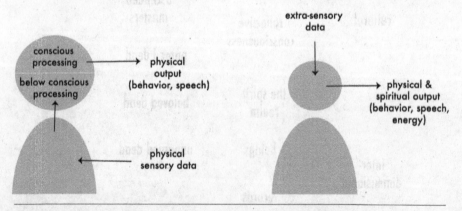

Diagrams of two common ways to understand how mediumship works.

Conceptual Frameworks

Embodied Mediumship Model

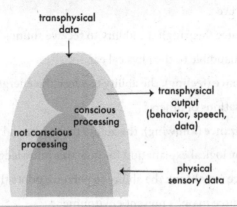

This hybrid conceptual model for embodied mediumship takes the entire human and their environment as part of the system facilitating connection and communication.

The Clairs

The first time I channeled information that the sitter confirmed in a mediumship message, I thought to myself, "Holy shit. I've been doing this my whole life." This is partly because mediumship is more than data from a spirit; the brain seamlessly integrates data from many sources. Another way to explain this is that I use claircognizance, or the ability to know things that cannot be logically explained. Psychic development work often focuses on "the clairs," offering another way to view how we may receive data. My first mediumship teacher, Dr. Judith Rochester, a Lily Dale Registered Medium Emeritus, calls the receptive instruments we use in mediumship the "soul senses."

Our brain is already wired to see, feel, taste, smell, and hear based on sensory input, so it makes sense that transphysical input could also be passed down those lines in the brain. There's a different quality to my soul's seeing—different from my imagination and memory—but the distinction is subtle. Just like we don't use a single sense, we use a combination of different clairs, and may have a favorite or dominant one. Here's an overview.

1. **Clairvoyance (seeing):** the ability to receive images, symbols, or scenes in the mind's eye
2. **Clairaudience (hearing):** the ability to receive sounds, words, or messages inaudible to the physical ear
3. **Clairsentience (feeling):** the ability to sense the energies, emotions, or bodily sensations of others
4. **Claircognizance (knowing):** the ability to understand information without any logical explanation for how this knowledge was acquired
5. **Clairalience (smelling):** the ability to perceive odors that don't have a physical source in one's present environment
6. **Clairgustance (tasting):** the ability to taste a substance without putting anything in one's mouth
7. **Clairtangency (touching):** also known as psychometry, is the ability to receive information about an object or person by touching or holding it
8. **Clairempathy (emotion):** the ability to experience the feelings of a contact
9. **Clairsalience (body sensation):** the ability to experience the bodily sensations of a contact

Making Something of the Data

I want to offer a case study to explore what happens after data have entered our minds and we have begun to work with it.

I was in my first year of training at Fellowships during one of the weekend-long intensives. I walked over every morning at eight for the half-hour *meditation* that started each session. On this particular morning, a few minutes into the meditation, I suddenly remembered closing my cat Athena in the bathroom and could not remember letting her back out. I concluded I had left her in there, and the moment the meditation ended, I ran out the door. As I turned onto my street, I looked up the hill toward my house and saw Nika sitting in the middle of the road. We walked up to the house, and the door wasn't latched, so I guessed it somehow flew open and she had gotten out. I ran to the back of the house, and the bathroom door was open. Athena slept upstairs.

I deduced that someone or something had sent me the message about Athena to get me home to put Nika back inside. I know that if I had received an image or message that Nika was running around the neighborhood I would have completely disregarded it—*not possible.* Leaving Athena in the bathroom was entirely possible since I had put her in there, and at the moment I got the message, I had no memory of letting her out.

I do not know where the data came from, but I do know it was a transphysical source because I sat in meditation when it occurred. The body uses whatever data it gets to set the state of our nervous system, and I was in an especially open, receptive state.

I had not moved my awareness to my house to clairvoyantly look at Athena in the bathroom, but I received, unbidden, an image of Athena in the bathroom. As I processed these data, I began to have bodily reactions that caused me to drop out of a meditative state and into anxiety.

I didn't notice then, but this was an odd response, because Athena wasn't in danger in the bathroom; she had only been there for maybe twenty minutes when I received the image. If I had received information about Nika's state, which was one of potential danger, it would have corresponded better to my response. The state created an emotion in me—it was some of the most arduous meditation I've done, thinking I needed to go home immediately.

It felt like the data (that I hadn't let Athena out of the bathroom) dropped directly into my brain. It combined with the information I already had (memory of Athena in the bathroom), my long-standing anxiety around caring for my animals, what constitutes a likely emergency, and what I am willing to believe. What I still find unnerving about this example is how smart whatever or whoever orchestrated all this messaging is.

I see two potential explanations: My body somehow received information that Nika was unsafe and produced an experience that would induce me to go home, where I could fix the situation. Or another being (potentially Athena or Nika) somehow delivered some information to my brain, which I happened to listen to. Some may suggest this was all a coincidence, a case of apophenia, or perceiving meaningful patterns in randomness, a form of bias that will be discussed further below. I cannot disprove this, but answer with Einstein's words, "Nature's laws are merely statements about temporal-spatial coincidences."

This illustrates some potentialities when we unintentionally engage—the importance of learning to turn off the capacity. It shows us how susceptible we are to manipulation. This is why we work to understand how our minds function and to distinguish when we imagine, deduce, remember, feel, or receive a mental experience. Learning not to grasp for or build ideas and our sources are two significant supports for this.

A Few Theories

There is so much unknown regarding the sensory data that our bodies and minds process, and attempting to add transphysical data veers us too deeply into unknown territory. However, some aspects of human psychology and neuroscience are well established enough to clarify our understanding of mediumship as data processing.

ACROSS THE HEMISPHERES

We are often taught that the two sides of the brain have a simple, clear delineation of tasks. This is contested by Dr. Iain McGilchrist's book, *The Master and His Emissary*, which has shown that the brain's two hemispheres help holistically with many aspects of cognition and behavior but could be understood as looking at the world from two different perspectives. McGilchrist posits that the left brain works by breaking up our experience into small pieces, and the right brain perceives a bigger scope through a wider lens. This creates a path from the right hemisphere, where we take in the entirety of our current experience, to the left hemisphere, where we break it into parts to make sense of each, and then back to the right hemisphere to put together the larger picture.

This is how I conceptualize receiving and processing data in mediumship sessions. First, after I've opened a connection, I use my right brain to focus on everything within that container. Then I allow certain features or elements, such as bodily sensations or clear visual images, to come to the foreground. Finally I look at all these elements together to communicate a coherent story for the sitter or my work.

BIASES AND DEFENSES

The mind is exceptional at processing quickly; to do that, it uses shortcuts, usually without conscious awareness. These shortcuts can be lifesaving (there's a car coming; I am already jumping away), they may be handy (there's a mosquito; I am already swatting it), irritating (I cannot stop blinking my eyes when the optometrist tries to put drops in them) or devastating (I heard a noise and shot at it before I could think).

These examples focus on the body, but the mind does the same, with a comparable spectrum of potential outcomes. As the body's reflexes can be lost or honed, the mind's shortcuts can be exposed, cultivated, or changed. Much of what we're learning for mediumship is to work with new data sources. Most of us aren't operating with our current data sources in perfect form, so it is worth the effort to revisit, reconsider, and maybe recondition some of our operational habits.

The challenges we have in the regular old corporeal world, with friends, colleagues, lovers, family, neighbors, and strangers, may repeat themselves in other realms because this is how our minds and bodies are habituated to operating. Noticing these trends helps illuminate where we need change. As hard as it is to hear that we've hurt someone's feelings, provided incorrect information, arrived at an unfair conclusion, or generally been found wrong, this information is precious. Each time, we can humbly accept the feedback and reflect on what happened, which improves our process the next time.

A few avenues that have been helpful for me to explore include the psychological concepts of biases and defense mechanisms. These theories identify processes that we develop to help us, at some point, avoid an undesirable feeling. These processes then become tools as we use them without conscious awareness, potentially mis- or overusing them. I consider them the most likely sources of inaccuracy and harm in mediumship because they lead us to insert our unquestioned assumptions into our data processing. The biases cropping up in myself most insidiously involve a tendency to discount data I receive that seem improbable or unpalatable. It takes constant effort to allow myself to see and bring forward this type of information, and my capacity to do so is my "frontier" in how much I can bring in from the beyond.

A Few Common Defense Mechanisms

- **Compartmentalization:** separating incompatible attitudes or behaviors into different domains
- **Compensation:** overachieving in one area to overcome deficiencies in another
- **Denial:** refusing to accept a painful reality
- **Displacement:** redirecting emotions from their source to a substitute target
- **Intellectualization:** overemphasizing logic to avoid emotional distress
- **Projection:** attributing one's unacceptable traits to others
- **Rationalization:** creating false but plausible reasons for one's actions
- **Reaction formation:** behaving oppositely to one's true feelings

Conceptual Frameworks

* **Regression:** reverting to childish behavior to avoid responsibility
* **Repression:** blocking unacceptable thoughts or impulses
* **Spiritual bypass:** using spiritual concepts to avoid unresolved or complex personal and societal problems
* **Sublimation:** channeling unacceptable impulses into socially acceptable behaviors

Common Biases (A Small Selection)

* **Anchoring:** the tendency to rely too heavily on the first piece of information presented when deciding
* **Apophenia:** perceiving meaningful patterns in something random
* **Availability:** judging probability by recalling examples
* **Confirmation:** the tendency to search for or interpret information in a way that confirms one's preconceptions
* **Egocentricity:** prioritizing one's own viewpoint
* **Extension neglect:** overlooking the size or extent of a problem or situation when making judgments or decisions
* **False priors:** using incorrect prior beliefs that influence the interpretation of new evidence, often leading to skewed conclusions
* **Framing effect:** drawing different conclusions from the same information when presented differently
* **Hindsight:** perceiving past events as having been more predictable than they actually were
* **Implicit:** unconscious attitudes or stereotypes toward other people
* **In-group:** favoring people who are like oneself
* **Negativity:** giving more weight to negative experiences than to positive ones
* **Optimism:** overestimating the likelihood of positive outcomes

Our unique blend of defense mechanisms and biases are specially crafted in the forge of our lives and are a significant part of what defines us. Psychologists recommend that when we discover one within ourselves, we get curious. We can't banish all these strategies. Still, we can acknowledge them, take time to accept that they exist for a reason, learn what needs they serve for us, understand how they work (which can include recalling when it has happened in the past and continuing to notice it in the future), thank them for keeping us alive, and begin to develop a new way to manage that kind of event or feeling in the future. This process is foundational in many types of therapy, and we may require the help of a professional or at least a friend to change our deep-seated ways of being in the world.

Output

You may be happy to know you already do this every single day. Anything can be an output mechanism: bodily movement, sounds, words, scribbles, songs. A simple option is a journal or voice memo folder for saving experiences each time they occur. Nothing complicated is needed—just do what you can to let it all out. There are many stories of mediums getting nagging messages that dissipated when they wrote them down.

Improvisation

Every time we sit down for mediumship, we bring our skills, experiences, wants, and needs. If we also bring a plan for the outcome, we miss the boat. Mediumship is about noticing what arises within a container we create for it. The more expectations we bring to the table, the more pressure and risk. Risk is the potential for danger. With its arrival, the connection goes. So mediumship asks us to engage with the process and let go of the outcome.

Every time, there is the potential for failure—this cannot be avoided. Every time, you may wonder, "Will it work?" And you will do your best, you will hope, and you will take those steps, not quite sure if there is a net to catch you as you sail off that cliff.

Charlie Parker said, "You've got to learn your instrument, then, you practice, practice, practice. And then, when you finally get up there on the bandstand, forget all that and just wail." Parker was a renowned musician who could improvise like no other. Mediumship is a constant, invisible interaction between the players—like improvisational music.

In his book *The Evolution of Imagination*, Stephen T. Asma identified critical features that enable improvisation. These features provide a fantastic way to summarize what happens in mediumship.

Freedom: a way of deciding between multiple behavioral options, without which many of these elements would be impossible. *Mediums are free to develop and evolve their own process.*

Imaginative faculties: a representational system to take experiences offline to process and make something new. *Mediums use their imagination to receive messages.*

Intuition: dependence on knowledge that is inherent, unconscious, or unempirical. *Mediums do not externally validate messages.*

Spontaneity: acting in real-time to create a seamless and natural generation of work. *Mediumship happens in the moment and isn't planned.*

Adaptation: a meaningful response to the environment. *Mediumship happens as an interaction between medium, contact, and their surroundings.*

Resource deficiency: as they say, necessity is the mother of invention. *Mediumship is done without our usual language faculties and physical senses.*

Self-imposed discipline: specific, strictly obeyed rules or protocols. *Through different traditions and contexts, mediumship has expectations and requirements for the medium.*

Simultaneous performance and composition: improvisation cannot be planned—the practice is the act. *Mediums use structures for readings, but there is no way to plan for what contacts will attend or what information they will bring through.*

Affective charge: a profound interplay between conscious feelings and the underlying physiological experiences of all those involved. *Mediumship is inherently relational and often confronts emotional issues of grief, love, and loss.*

High-stakes conditions: improvisers overcome the natural desire to turn away from vulnerability by regularly putting themselves in scenarios where they will face that fear. *Message work, readings, and public demonstrations ask mediums to perform their skills for strangers without prior planning.*

Importance of reliable clichés: scaffolding for the improviser to bring out at the right time, like the musician's signature riff and the comedian's favorite impersonations. *Mediums often use specific language, find trends in the topics they work with, and build certain types of guidance into their readings.*

These three aspects of improvisation are less obviously relevant to mediumship, but just as useful.

Functional promiscuity: a way of doing things rather than domain-specific knowledge. *This is the premise of this book: we can use mediumship for anything.*

Mixing frames: bringing together disparate systems and conventions that allow new meaning to emerge. *This is how we expand mediumship and continue its evolution, as I do with improvisation and data processing.*

Humor: a self-reflexive awareness of the process that helps reduce the tension of all this novelty. *Mediums could use more of this!*

Improvisation is a flexible practice that creates an imperfect but engaging work made with elastic rules. When we view mediumship through this lens rather than "practice makes perfect," we get closer to understanding what we're doing here. For this reason, mediums bristle if you call mediumship a performance—genuine mediumship is unique in every instance, and there is no revising of what happens in a session.

Clowning

During the pandemic, I learned about clowning. It sounded like my nightmare—goofy, unrestrained—but people said it was cathartic, and I saw how its darkness and laughter were missing in my life of Spiritualist mediumship, which is so focused on lightness and crying. So I took an online class through The Clown School. With groups of strangers, some wildly talented, I put on a red clown nose (really!) and practiced exaggerating my body to show—rather than tell—the absurdity of life and get people to laugh.

I was not an effective clown. I was, however, confronted with one of the biggest reasons we want to control mediumship—that we are socialized not to appear foolish. Clowning is essentially making foolish look good. It helped me get comfortable with the fact that I do something inherently strange, marginal, and nonsensical when practicing mediumship. An act that cannot be predetermined or ensured. I learned what improvisation entailed and saw its application to mediumship. That improvisational nature of the practice is doubled when you have an audience, even of one.

Interviewing

I often joke that I have two careers: a "rational" one in research and design and an "irrational" one in mediumship. The two may seem very different at first glance. Looking deeper, they both rely on my ability to connect with others, to listen, and to be able to synthesize what I learn into reliable, tangible, usable output. Although I engage in the same activities in many cases, one is considered smart and sensible, and the other is considered "woo-woo." Sometimes, when I explain mediumship as a form of interviewing—one of the tools I use for research—people can more readily see the similarities.

In my human-computer interaction studies, we learned how to program computers and how to study humans and their needs to make better choices in our programs. The methods I learned were called "human-centered design," which focused on iterative phases of data collection, synthesis, and prototyping solutions through interviewing, observing, surveying, and collaborating with the people for whom we designed programs. Although I no longer focus on only software, I still use all these methods (even in writing this book!) and have conducted thousands of interviews throughout my career. It has made me a better medium for my sitters and contacts.

Here's how that process works for me:

1. Preparation

* **Define objectives:** Outline the goals of the interview. What questions are we looking to answer?
* **Identify participants:** Choose interviewees who can represent the people we are studying.
* **Develop a guide:** Create a discussion guide with open-ended questions aligned with our objectives.
* **Logistics:** Schedule the interview at a convenient time and location for the participant, ensuring a quiet and comfortable setting.

2. Building Rapport

* **Introduction:** Introduce yourself and explain the purpose of the interview. Help the participant feel comfortable and valued.
* **Consent:** Obtain informed consent, explain how the data will be used, and ensure confidentiality.
* **Warm-up questions:** Start with easy, nonthreatening questions to help the participant relax.

3. Conducting the Interview

* **Active listening:** Pay constant attention to the participant's responses with genuine curiosity and understanding.
* **Open-ended questions:** Avoid yes-or-no questions to encourage detailed responses and learn the participant's thoughts and feelings.
* **Follow-up probes:** Ask follow-up questions to clarify or expand on interesting points. Use prompts like, "Can you tell me more about that?" or "Why do you think that is?"
* **Stay neutral:** Avoid leading questions and remain impartial to prevent influencing the participant's responses.

4. Closing the Interview

* **Summarize:** Briefly summarize key points to ensure understanding and allow the participant to clarify or add information.
* **Final thoughts:** Ask if there is anything else the participant would like to share.
* **Thank-you:** Express gratitude for their time and insights. Inform them of any next steps or how they can access the results, if applicable.

Beyond

A mediumship reading is an interview between the medium and the contact, where the sitter is the audience. The only part of the process we leave out are any post-interview activities because, unlike research interviews, only the sitter collects the information in a reading. While this standardized process can apply to most forms of interviews, such as mediumship, we need singular focus and improvisation skills to have the best possible conversation. These skills are highly transferrable between the material and spiritual worlds or between rational and irrational careers.

---

1. What is mediumship? When you read the first chapter, what did you decide about mediumship? Do you have any new theories of what is going on yet?

2. Have you had any experiences that added to your understanding or shifted your interests?

3. Regard a living, other-than-human being. Consider how it takes in data, processes it, and outputs a response to the world.

DEVELOPING YOUR UNDERSTANDING

1. **Map your boggle threshold:** Write short descriptions of your foundational experiences around spirituality, the uncanny, and anomalous phenomena on index cards. Order them in time, and on the back of each card write how that experience affected your beliefs about what is real, what humans are capable of, and what matters in life. Next write a few more cards with beliefs you aren't convinced of yet, putting them in order from the one you feel closest to accepting to those that seem far-fetched. Then turn the new cards over and imagine what could happen that would convince you. Write that possibility (or a few) on the blank cards. If you move your boggle threshold, trade out the imagined version for a new card with what you experience.

2. **Chart your sources:** Print out the sources map and take it to your next conversation with another living person. As you talk, circle the sources you notice you use to hold the conversation. When you see one that is missing, add it in. Don't worry too much about putting it in the correct location on the chart, but return to it after the conversation to see if there are other categories of sources you used and would like to add.

3. **Prepare an interview** for a living person whom you'd like to get to know better. Then prepare an interview for a dead person. Notice the differences in how you feel about the two interviews and where you make assumptions or feel limited. Interview the living person, then try it with the dead person. You can have the living person pretend to be the dead person, you can pretend to be the dead person, or you can imagine the dead person is responding to your questions.

CHAPTER 3
BEING A RESPONSIBLE MEDIUM

During my first few months in Lily Dale, or just "the Dale" if you're local, I often wondered if my neighbors were reading my mind. I'd be walking the dog, someone would wave, and I'd cringe, thinking they knew how much I didn't like the color of their house. Busy with yard work one afternoon, I stopped to watch a neighbor unloading groceries. I saw a pineapple sticking out of a bag and thought how good that sounded, making a mental note to get more fruit the next time I went to the store, before continuing with my raking. A few seconds later, my neighbor interrupted me with a glass jar of fruit cocktail in her extended hand. "Would you like this?" I answered slowly, looking her right in the eye to see if she'd give some hint that she'd heard my thoughts and was responding to them directly. With no such nonverbal acknowledgment, I said yes and thanked her profusely.

Once I began to hone my psychic skills, it seemed cute that I worried people in Lily Dale were intentionally reading minds all the time. The practice takes focus and effort—things people rarely expend without a good reason. But many people read minds by accident, as my neighbor did. The fruit was an innocent and positive example. Many unsolicited psychic occurrences are not. When I tell people I work as a medium, they often respond with stories of strangers coming up to them in the grocery store with messages from their dead loved ones or psychics who told them they were going to have some wildly accurate or inaccurate number of babies. One of my favorite aspects of Lily Dale is that nearly everyone here has been taught at least the basic foundational ethics around mediumship, and you will rarely encounter these faux pas.

Having spent many formative years in a part of California known for its hippie culture, I have been aware of the downsides of being involved in "woo" since a young age. I decided early that I wanted to make sure I wasn't the kind of person who made others feel unsafe, spied on, less than, or taken advantage of—or, conversely, one who took on the pain of others or had clients knocking on their doors all hours of the day and night. I had mostly decided I'd do this by not giving readings, but as I started to get to know many professionals, I came to see that it is possible to do this work without harming others or myself.

One of the most common questions about mediumship is if it is safe. In popular media, we see mediums experience evil spirits, involuntary *possession*, angry *ghosts*, murderous zombies, and many more terrifying transliving others. Even the few in-depth portrayals of mediums in media that aren't meant to be scary, like in the movies *Hereafter* and *Vibes,* mediumship is depicted as uncontrollable and unsafe. Modern American Spiritualism (the source of the bulk of my formal mediumship education) acknowledges that death doesn't inherently produce goodness yet assumes if a spirit is coming through, they are coming with love. There is a lot of power in focusing on positivity, which works for most Spiritualists. When I first moved to Lily Dale and learned this perspective, I started using the word *ghostism* to explain the pervasive stereotype of transliving beings as bad in media. However, it isn't as simple as all bad, all good, all safe, or all dangerous.

I sought out initiates and teachers of traditions of regional and diaspora religions from Europe, Africa, and the Americas. My early teacher Marza Millar and later Andrea Wadsworth, a gifted seer, diviner, healer, and medium whom I worked with one on one for several years, taught me a more balanced approach that helped me feel safe working outside the confines of Spiritualist mediumship. From them, I learned that the spirit world encompasses many forms of being, as in our human world. Some seek to harm, some hurt and cannot help but hurt others, and some seek healing and growth for all—the whole gamut runs throughout existence here, hereafter, and everywhere in between.

Being aware of and preparing for challenges does not make them more likely to happen, just as we cannot simply make good things happen by hoping for the best. We can think of this as preparation for travel to a country very different from our own. In general, the same rules apply when we're at home. However, in this place, we don't quite have the same understanding of how things work, when to be cautious, and how to find help. Developing discernment, boundaries, and other safety protocols will help us decide when, where, and with whom we work to serve our values and potential best.

In addition to external safety, we must consider our internal environment. There is a genuine potential for delusion in these practices. Most of us have spent our whole lives unlearning *intuition*, a connection to our bodies and souls, nature, or any other sort of higher power or unknowable realms. This means we lack practical knowledge, which reduces our capacity for discernment. Remembering how much these things mean to us and how far we've wandered from them can create a natural longing. We can trick ourselves if we try to move too quickly, ignore complications, or wander off too far alone.

Mediumship allows us to look at what is unseen in our world. This can include feelings, experiences, ideas, and traits in ourselves that we don't want to see. If we fail to address what comes up in this practice, we can become susceptible to avoidance behaviors, such as substance abuse and spiritual bypassing.

The tools offered in this book are only a start to becoming a responsible medium. We also need respect, dedication, awareness, accountability, and honesty. Cultivating ethics and safety are foundational to these efforts, as is knowing when to get help. We all need guidance and support. There are times to reach out to a loved one or a professional. Prepare for this by developing a support list of people and organizations you would feel comfortable calling on for physical, emotional, spiritual, and mental care. There are a few places to start in the resources toward the end of the book.

Ethics

In addition to keeping ourselves safe and healthy, this practice requires us always to consider the health and safety of others. For an uncommonly clear and thorough understanding of the ethical considerations of mediumship, please read *Ethics in Energy Medicine* by Heidi Light, who has almost thirty years of experience as a counselor in private, clinical, and institutional settings and over fifty years as a medical intuitive, empath, and energy tracker. She offers the foundations needed for practitioners to ensure they do no harm by expanding the model of ethics taught to counselors and psychologists with her understanding of intuitive and energetic work, all in a short and easy-to-read format. I used her pillar framework to create my code of conduct, an ever-evolving document on my website.

Ethical Pillar: Informed Consent and Permission

My promise to sitters: I don't connect before our session or until you've given me a verbal okay. In psychic work, I will connect only with you and your energy.

My promise to contacts: I won't come looking for you or require you to connect. I only work with those who willingly come to me. I do not connect to living humans without verbal consent.

Confidentiality and Privacy

Sitters: You are welcome to receive an anonymous reading. I strive to keep all information of your appointments, including the existence of appointments in the first place, strictly between me and you. Please do not look up my personal information or attempt to contact me except regarding an appointment.

Contacts: You are welcome not to identify yourself, but I may not be able to connect without sufficient information to determine my safety. I am available for connection only during mediumship and do not allow contacts to drop in.

Supervision and Professional Associations

Sitters: I am actively working on my growth and healing with practitioners much more experienced than myself. I focus on bimonthly sessions with a counselor and monthly *development circles* with other experienced mediums. I am currently an ordained minister at Fellowships of the Spirit.

Contacts: I work with a *gatekeeper* and an ever-growing team of mentors, teachers, ancestors, and guides in transphysical reality.

Scope of Practice and Delivery of Service

Sitters: I am not a doctor or therapist, and my work is not a replacement for these professionals. Our time together is short, and I strive for timeliness—I hope you do, too. I cannot reschedule or refund an appointment on the same day. However, if you are unhappy with the reading, let me know in the first ten minutes, and I'll refund you.

Contacts: I ask that you speak to me in ways I can understand. I will do my best to convey your message, but I am not the right medium for all contacts.

Objectivity and Not Giving Advice

Sitters: I aim to provide unconditional support to everyone I work with. You are your own healer, and I'm here to help you with that. I may offer some ideas for things you can do, but I aim to share information, not give advice.

Contacts: I will offer your message to my sitter as clearly and accurately as I can. I reserve the right to edit, condense, or not pass on information that I believe would harm the sitter.

Appropriate Recordkeeping and Charging of Fees

Sitters: If you would like your session recorded, please ask. I keep scheduling records (including payment receipts) but no other types of records. I charge for my time at industry-standard rates. If payment is ever a barrier for you, please reach out. I am happy to find another form of reciprocity.

Contacts: I offer reciprocity to all my contacts by delivering messages to you from the sitter, offering attention and understanding, and, in some cases, altar work or other support in physical form. Please let me know what reciprocity feels right to you, and I will do my best to comply.

Attention and Choice

Sitters: When we start your reading, I will open the connection and my attention will stay with you until our session ends. A lot of effort is required to focus on multiple realms, and I can only do so for you during our sessions. Know that I practice safe connection through prayerful request, grounding, energetic hygiene, and mindfulness.

Contacts: I am grateful to all my contacts for their efforts. As a freely chosen connection, you are welcome to leave at any time. If I ask you to leave or change how we work together, please respect my decision.

Process and Connection

Sitters: You can expect that I do any experimental work outside our sessions—unless you ask for it! This is not a hard science—my process is constantly evolving, and if you have ideas for something you'd like to try, let me know. I am also happy to explain what is going on during a session; please feel free to ask.

Contacts: If there are ways I can strengthen the connection while we are working together, please elaborate. I reserve the right to use my existing techniques and try your suggestions at another time, depending on the sitter and my needs.

Safety

Developing the ability to reach into the spirit realm may seem like the main challenge we face in becoming mediums, but it is not. Safety is paramount to our capacity as mediums, not because this work is significantly more dangerous than other forms of communication but because it is considerably harder to do when we do not feel safe. Exploring how we experience safety from a neurological standpoint can help us improve our ability to feel safe.

Our ability to do mediumship—and anything else—depends on our physical, emotional, mental, and spiritual state. These states all change from moment to moment. We can discern if we feel ready for mediumship on a particular day or moment by connecting to these aspects of our beings and heeding what we find there.

One way of understanding our readiness is to consider our state of consciousness. This is usually discussed within the context of altered states of consciousness, also called non-ordinary states. In Western circles until the 1960s, they were not associated with science but with demonic possession or intoxication. Although states of consciousness are now studied by many, the scientific, philosophical, and religious communities have not come to a consensus among themselves or across groups. For our purposes, we generally refer to synthesizing our physical, emotional, mental, and spiritual condition into a single state.

States of consciousness are often categorized as ordinary or non-ordinary, meaning something that feels like regular life or something different. Mediumship practices are typically considered only psychic connection, which could be viewed as a non-ordinary state. This is an important part of the practice but is not always possible or advisable for everyone. I have experimented with a wide array of states using various means. For me, mediumship most comfortably sits in a barely non-ordinary state, like being very focused or relaxed. Even my most impactful and far-out mediumship experiences happened in a state very close to, if not entirely, ordinary. So mediumship remains accessible to those who aren't able or willing to engage in non-ordinary states. To account for both types of mediumship, we will refer to it as transordinary, including both ordinary and non-ordinary states. To this end, I've included exercises for both states, focusing on using presence, movement, performance, creativity, and imagination to connect in an ordinary state.

An appropriate condition for transordinary mediumship is one where I am aware enough to have the capacity to determine and navigate my state. Our state can be changed without our control by our nervous system or with our controlled focus. Even deep introspection can change our state, as can everyday activities: sleeping, daydreaming, breathwork, *dissociation*, exercise, music, sex, hypnosis, submerging the body in water, and conversation. Sleep and dreaming offer an everyday experience in state changing. I have spent a lot of time cultivating the ability to change state during the moments before I fall asleep or come awake, called the *hypnagogic state*.

Lots of less common activities can also shift our state: dementia, psychosis, fasting, sleep deprivation, near-death experiences, seizures, and comas. And, of course, plenty of substances, legal and not, can alter our consciousness. For mediumship, we need to learn to control going in and out of our ordinary state. This starts by understanding what feels like an ordinary state for us. This may not be possible for all people all the time. If we are in a period where we cannot find an ordinary state, are struggling to determine what state we are in, or are moving between states in a way we cannot control, it is time for activities that focus on ordinary states in the material realm.

A friend, artist, and medium who struggles with her mental health described her challenges in a way that feels accurate for conditions like depression, anxiety, schizophrenia, and even grief: " . . . the information [I take in during mediumship] can become skewed or delusional when I am unwell. It has taken years, and I am still sorting out the line between 'real and unreal.'"

Similarly, using a substance or inducing a physical condition to find a transordinary state won't allow most of us to maintain the control we need to leave the state at will or change the level of intensity of the shift. This renders such paths inappropriate for mediumship in most cases. I recommend that readers who employ recreational consciousness-altering substances (including alcohol, marijuana, and, when working with high levels of sensitivity, even caffeine) not overlap their use and this practice. For those who work within traditions and with the support of experts using substances or physical conditions to reach transordinary states, always use care and discernment when combining protocols or practices from various sources.

I cannot provide guidance on medical conditions, and I do not recommend changing any medical treatment based on reading this book. If medication is used to maintain an ordinary state of consciousness, consulting a professional before trying to change states is essential. We'll develop a spectrum of less-ordinary states based mostly on closing your eyes and focusing your attention, so they should be compatible with many conditions and medications.

It is important to recognize that currently, there is no functional clinical understanding of mediumship or other anomalous phenomena. The Emergent Phenomenology Research Consortium works to remedy this situation while acknowledging a lack of shared language for understanding what happens during mediumship. Further, most health-care workers not only lack training in supporting it or related practices and experiences but may not know what it is. This makes finding health care a challenge if there is an emergency. Even for those with no mental or physical health concerns, mediumship amplifies the need for a strong personal support network and meticulous attention to our state before and while engaging.

There are also plenty of circumstances that can make transordinary states unwise or impractical. Many people face physical, emotional, and energetic harm every day. Many have little to no control over the people in their lives or environmental settings because of temporary or permanent conflict, incarceration, institutionalization, incapacitation, confinement, or limited access to financial resources. This may necessitate sticking with ordinary states for mediumship, waiting until circumstances change, working in groups, working for very short periods, and working on long-term plans to find safe places to practice. Building up even tiny moments of safety and connection *is* doing the work.

UNCOMFORTABLE VERSUS UNSAFE

Running up a slippery hill in the woods with my dog Nika's son Coyo one day, panting, muscles burning, I felt myself hurting. Should I stop? My answer, at that moment, was no. I want to be stronger. I want to run farther. I have more in me. Things are much less apparent with emotional discomfort and in situations where we do not have a choice. Sometimes there is a fine line between dangerous and difficult; sometimes we confuse the two. It is up to us to decide every single time we experience pain or discomfort. Since life often gives us the hard things, in this work can we seek out the glimmer over the struggle?

Tools for Cultivating Safety

There are times, places, contacts, and situations that do not call for mediumship. Many of us also have inner work to prepare our minds and bodies for safe, reliable, and nourishing connection.

State Change

Simply because we have determined that we have a level of physical and psychological security that we believe is appropriate for mediumship doesn't mean our physiology will comply. To understand what we can do if we find ourselves stuck in feelings of danger, I refer to *polyvagal theory*, developed by Dr. Stephen W. Porges, a distinguished scientist and psychiatry professor, the founding director of the Traumatic Stress Research Consortium, and former president of the Society for Psychophysiological Research and the Federation of Associations in Behavioral & Brain Sciences. His research began in the late 1960s, and he has written over 400 publications to date. This work has been expanded by scientists in dozens of fields and used by clinicians to develop innovative treatments for behavioral, psychiatric, and physical disorders.

Polyvagal theory explains that our nervous system constantly monitors our external environment for safety and risk to produce three involuntary or autonomic states that profoundly influence our behavior. This scanning of our external environment for cues of safety and danger is called neuroception, and it occurs below our conscious control. When danger is perceived, our nervous system prepares by changing critical bodily functions, including heart rate, digestion, and breathing, which limits our behavioral options.

A very simplified way of looking at the two defensive states is that mobilization (fight or flight) prepares us to move: our heart rate increases, we are on alert, and we may feel anxious or jumpy. Immobilization (freeze) reduces our capacity to move and engage, depressing our heart rate and shutting us down.

In both states, we lose access to what we find in the non-defensive third state called social engagement: connection, empathy, learning, creativity, play, intimacy, rest, recovery, problem-solving, and many other capacities we want and need. Accessing this state and its broader behavioral options is not only useful for mediumship; it is a foundational part of mental and physical health. Connection and co-regulation with our fellow humans are not simply a nice thing to have but a biological imperative—we cannot live without them.

I divide the social engagement state to suggest it has a transordinary nature. The ordinary substate gives us increased access to cognition with the focus, logic, and problem-solving at which humans are exceptional. With the right conditions, I find a transordinary state that could be understood as having psychic elements, flow, or transcendence. This is where the thinking mind turns off and we find access to connection beyond ourselves. In polyvagal theory, this is associated with compassion and not separated as distinctly as I am describing. This isn't the only place mediumship happens, but it is a highly receptive state that facilitates information to which our logical minds might not have access or understanding.

The defensive states are sometimes referred to as dysregulation, and the non-defensive state of social engagement is considered regulation. This is somewhat misleading because all states are necessary for survival in certain circumstances. The ability to fight, flee, and hide from danger has kept our species alive and is not bad or undesirable in many situations. The problem arises if we are stuck in a defensive state when we don't need it. This can happen because the nervous system responds to present cues in part using past experience. A nervous system that incorrectly determines us to be in danger can keep us from accessing the benefits of the social engagement state. This can have severe consequences for our health—and can be caused by physiological and psychological illnesses and differences, as well as *trauma* and harm.

Beyond

Polyvagal theory recognizes that many of us have significant challenges to overcome to cultivate safety. These are physiological—not psychological—states of the body and are due to a reflexive response to our environment. We cannot choose them. Hunger or tiredness are also internal states over which we have little direct control. Our tendency to go into one state or another can change over time and is influenced by our actions, experiences, and genetics. At times our entire culture seems to be suffering from near-constant dysregulation because we live in a world of so much stress from systems that are not conducive to our biological needs for safety and connection, compounded by *intergenerational trauma*, which is passed down in both behavior and DNA.

Like hunger or tiredness, after we recognize our neurological state, we can respond in ways that change how we feel. As Deb Dana, LCSW, a clinician specializing in helping people explore and resolve trauma, says, we can "retune

	Freeze	Fight or Flight	Social Engagement	Flow
Physical Sensations	exhaustion, numbness, incapacitation	heat, rapid heartbeat, shaking	awareness of time, space, self, others	oneness with time, space, self, others
Emotions	nothingness, shutdown, confusion	rage, fear, panic	calm, curiosity, empathy	bliss, love, joy
Behaviors	dissociation, slowness, avoidance	violence, hurrying, hyper-vigilance	communication, curiosity, focus	inspiration, connection, compassion
Abilities	defensive immobilization	defensive mobilization	problem-solving, logic, learning	creativity, intimacy, play

Neurological states, plus flow, and potential experiences within each.

neuroception and reshape habitual responses." I know this is true because I have and continue to do so. I first learned how to notice when I felt safe through the skills I developed in mediumship, and studying polyvagal theory gave me the language for and understanding of why it all worked.

If we want to practice mediumship and find ourselves in a defensive state, we can check if we are in danger. If so, we are in the correct nervous system state and must attend to the situation. If not, we can identify the cause of the defensive state outside us and then attempt to move locations to support a state shift. If we determine the cause is internal, we can check if it is due to a physical issue, and again we need to address the situation. To put simply: we shouldn't try to shift our state if we are in danger. This is more obvious with explicit factors, but it also applies to the primary care of our bodies.

Listening to the Body

Whether or not we feel safe *within* our body, or implicit safety, is a complex amalgamation of our genetics, experiences, and environment. Explicit constraints, including the needs of the other people in our lives, jobs, and environment, create a tension between what our bodies tell us and what we must do. Even after we have removed explicit dangers, we often have implicit factors that keep us feeling unsafe.

This is true even for those who have not experienced trauma. Seemingly innocuous, ordinary acts taught to many primary schoolers, such as not eating when hungry (wait for snack time) or not going to the bathroom when we need to (wait until break time), can establish a wall between the mind and body. Harmful social constructs of racial hierarchy, beauty standards, gender bias, ableism, and other external pressures can make it difficult or impossible for us to listen to our bodies to keep ourselves physically and emotionally safe.

ECHOES OF TIME

This is a zooming-out practice that helps me remind myself that I am not in control of my neurological state and that myriad forces are acting upon me at any time. You will need a large piece of paper and a writing instrument. First, write down your current feelings. Then, zoom out from the current moment: what has been influencing you for the past few minutes? Hours? Weeks? Decades? Millenia? For each time frame, posit what might have contributed to your current state.

Notice how unclear the potential influences become as we look further back in time and complexity builds up. After you zoom out, ask yourself, what state are you in right now? What do the different states feel like in your body? Start a diary of when you find yourself in different states, what it is like, and what bodily experience helps you know you are in it.

One of the most potent parts of learning mediumship included reconnecting with my body. By noticing the sensations happening in our bodies and the different ways we talk to ourselves, we may find a parent's voice admonishing us or an internalized expression of society keeping us in line. We may have an inner meanie who creates a tense atmosphere that cannot be escaped. When we don't, or can't, listen to our bodies' needs, whether ignoring hunger or fullness, getting too much or too little sleep or rest, getting too much or too little exercise, restricting access to certain things we love to eat or do or be, part of us thinks that is the best way for us to survive. However, ignoring these bodily cues produces an experience of danger within the body, making it impossible to move out of a defensive state.

In addition to polyvagal theory, Dr. Robert M. Sapolsky's *Determined* looks at the many ways in which we have less control over our behavior than we think.

SELF-SOOTHSAYER DECK

Make a tool to help when you need ideas for changing your state. Get a deck of cards and a thick permanent marker. You can make the deck bottom up: each time you notice you are dysregulated, ask yourself what you need, and before you take action, write the soothing act on the front of one of the cards. Or you can do this top down: make a big list of all the things you use to soothe yourself. Consider classic tools for shifting your autonomic state: humming, deep breathing, rocking, shaking, singing, chanting, sweeping, or other gentle repetitive body movements. Add in your own, like putting on socks, having a snack, or saying your name three times. Write one on each card, and perhaps split them up by "suit," with ideas for soothing the heart, mind, body, or spirit. Also include things you can do with others (court cards) and alone.

Self-soothe space: Develop a ritual to use when doing mediumship, mindfulness, creativity, or any exercises in this book. This may include going to a specific place, dimming the lights, or using headphones or earplugs. It might need to happen during a particular time of day when you are alone. You may want to ensure certain scents or temperatures. You may have a person to co-regulate with. When you have created this space, check in with yourself: Using the chart from page 52, can you identify your state based on how you are thinking and feeling? If you spend all your time simply finding a moment of ease, you've done enough. If you are consistently struggling to feel the sensations, emotions, or behaviors associated with safety, try changing some of the variables you've chosen, or consider enlisting a professional to help you. Some counselors and therapists understand polyvagal theory and can support your development of self-regulation. You don't need to do this alone!

Although we would all like to think our rational minds and free will keep us the good people we are, there is an increasing body of evidence that our physiological state is made up of influences ranging from the immediate back throughout human existence, the vast majority of which we have no control over. This revelation is less for relinquishing responsibility for our actions and more to recognize interconnectedness and identify our limitations, granting grace to ourselves and others, and making the most of where we feel we have control. These tasks are relevant and essential for mediumship.

Co-regulation

Our nervous systems pay attention to our surroundings and the nervous systems of other beings in our proximity. Being around a person in a defensive state is enough for some nervous systems to move into a defensive state themselves. The reverse is also true; if a person is in a social engagement state, they may help others become regulated merely by being near them. This capacity, called co-regulation, is one of the primary functions disrupted by trauma, resulting in difficulties in establishing and maintaining relationships. When co-regulation is impaired, working with other mammals, who also have a social engagement state, may provide a path back to co-regulation. I find singing with others one of the most enjoyable co-regulation activities. However, I find it highly agitating if I'm in a group where we cannot find harmony.

It isn't quite the same as co-regulation with another nervous system, but studies have found that connection to nature is restorative and can help shift the nervous system. When access to the outdoors isn't possible, even indoor plants or looking at images of a natural setting can have a regulating effect.

Movement

We don't always need to figure out why we are dysregulated, struggling, or just out of sorts. I can sometimes recognize my state by an intense need to research something or when I launch into scout mode, aggressively trying to figure myself out. I find that information and mental engagement soothe me at times, which I've heard called "flurry" or "facts" as a substate of fight or flight. However, this often turns into a circular mess, and I get increasingly agitated at being unable to solve the issue. In these moments, I return to my body through movement (if I'm closer to flight or fight) or imagining movement (if I'm closer to freeze). Clinician Deb Dana's book *Polyvagal Exercises for Safety and Connection* is a fantastic guide for how to support state change consciously.

Physical and imagined (transphysical) movement are ways to shift the nervous system. Whenever I mention movement throughout the book, know that both are an option. Start with a movement that feels good in the moment and repeat it—walking, pacing, shaking, dancing, punching the air, flapping, mobility drills, closing and opening the eyes, stretching, rocking. Notice the speed that feels comfortable and consider shifting it faster or slower. Sometimes simply changing the speed of motion of current activity is enough to help the nervous system rebalance.

This doesn't need to be a regular practice, and it is not for exercise—this is for intentionally allowing the body to move when and how it desires to shape the nervous system. Exercise can be regulating for some, especially gentle types in calm surroundings, like canoeing or walking. It can also be used to learn to enter and exit stress states, like through weight lifting or interval training. Know that increased heart and breathing rates can feel like dysregulation, making more strenuous exercise feel like too much for an already stressed body.

The Breath

Breath is a powerful tool for recognizing and shifting state. I use it daily, both outside and within my mediumship practice, to help me center, shift between activities, stay calm, and focus, especially when life gets in the way: a shock right before a reading, not feeling well, a client who makes me more nervous than usual, or a crowd all looking at me.

Beyond

We breathe every minute of every day and only need to focus on it for a tiny percentage of that time to work with it. Breathwork typically uses a few different ways to focus on how the body breathes in and out:

* **Ratios:** how long inhales, holds, and exhales last compared with each other
* **Pacing:** matching breaths to specific frequencies, shapes like a box, or rhythms like a wave
* **Bodily engagement:** using only part of the body to breathe—like one nostril at a time—or shifting between belly and chest breathing
* **Vocalization:** humming, toning, buzzing, sighing, and singing can all be soothing to the nervous system
* **And resulting state changes:** patterns that shift the breather into a particular state

The combination of ratio, pace, vocalization, and bodily engagement will determine the state change, summarized into two major types:

Soothing Breaths
Focus on the exhale to make it longer than the inhale. Use these breaths when feeling off, dysregulated, or agitated. They will help the nervous system settle into a calm and connected state. A subset that mimics the natural breath pattern of sleep (exhale for twice as long as inhale) is lovely for bedtime.

These patterns help downregulate the nervous system from a mobilized state. This releases neurotransmitters that relax muscles, slow heart rate, engage metabolism and energy storage, and reduce stress hormones. In addition to their immediate relaxation effects, these patterns demonstrate health benefits over long periods of use.

GET TO KNOW YOUR BREATH

Download a breathing app with beautiful music, engaging visual indicators, various breathing patterns, and games to keep you coming back. Find one you like and experiment with the different types of breathwork.

Try a breathwork circle or otherwise facilitated group breathing session. Kundalini and other types of yoga incorporate breathwork. If you are interested in altered states, try a holotropic breathwork class with a facilitator. It is a powerful way to experience psychedelic states without substances and with the ability to stop the effect at any time by changing the rate and type of breath.

Find a bodywork practitioner who can help you explore and understand your breath. The Resources section includes a list of people I've worked with.

Activating Breaths

The reverse focuses on the inhale and increasing the intensity and pace. These patterns help with focus, getting out of bed in the morning, improving clarity, and preparing for activity. More intense versions can move the breather into a transordinary state.

These patterns can help stimulate the nervous system out of an immobilized state. Because we control the state shift, we can experience the positive effects of overcoming the minor stress of shortened breaths. This heightens alertness, speeds up heart rate, and makes us feel energized. Over time, they can increase the body's ability to manage and recover from stress and improve energy and focus.

Discernment

Discernment is the ability to recognize, distinguish, and interpret different data sources and assess the validity and relevance of the received data. More simply, it is how we make decisions. Working within our internal experience removes us from the comforts of social approval, scientific proof, and common sense. We're left alone with our wits and must find ways to trust ourselves.

Respondents to my survey identified discernment as a skill developed over time through experience, often involving a combination of sensory cues, intuitive feelings, and rational analysis to navigate the complex landscape of transphysical communication. Its use involves several key aspects:

1. **Differentiating sources:** We use discernment to distinguish between different types of contacts (e.g., spirits, guides, ancestors) and sources of information.
2. **Validating information:** Discernment helps assess whether the information received is relevant and accurate.
3. **Assessing intent and quality:** We use discernment to evaluate the nature and intent of the contact, distinguishing between benevolent and potentially harmful sources.
4. **Recognizing energetic signatures:** Many of us feel different energies or frequencies with various sources and use this to identify the origin of the information.
5. **Filtering personal bias:** Discernment separates thoughts, emotions, and biases from externally received information.
6. **Pattern recognition:** Over time we develop the ability to recognize patterns in how different sources communicate, enhancing our identification skills.

7. **Managing mental health:** Discernment is crucial in interpreting our state and if experiences are from external sources or internal responses.
8. **Interpreting symbolic or abstract information:** Discernment helps us understand and translate non-literal or metaphoric messages.
9. **Maintaining boundaries:** Discernment identifies the need for boundaries to establish which communications to engage with and which to filter out.

Mediumship is like traveling, as it allows us to get out of our comfort zone. This also means it takes a lot of energy. When I visit a new place, especially where I do not speak the language, it takes extra effort to do the most basic things, like eat, sleep, and care for myself. I do not have a home filled with food and clothing in case I can't find what I need out in the world. My energies are spent like a nomadic hunter; there's not always much left for creativity or compassion. I must learn to care for myself differently, and depending on how far I am from home physically, culturally, and linguistically, I may have few guardrails left.

When the scaffolding of my daily life and culture has been stripped away, I see what of myself is me. This involves a lot of discernment. Even little things like deciding between two restaurants can have significant consequences—will it end up giving me food poisoning or being the best meal of my life? But are the stakes that high most of the time? Finding ways to reduce the pressure we put on ourselves allows us to make better decisions.

One of the most common uses for *divination* tools and professional psychics is when we can't decide on something. This often happens because we're receiving conflicting information from various sources. There are a few things I do in this case, whether I am dealing with a mundane decision or while doing mediumship:

1. Gather more information. A few potential sources: divinations, calling a friend (or, if in the mediumship process, calling another contact), asking a professional, and internet research.
2. Meditate, let my mind wander, or take my mind off the issue with something relaxing or enjoyable.
3. Move my attention to my body (including individual parts like the gut or heart), mind, and spirit to see how their responses differ.
4. Wait. Take a breath.
5. Ask a different question or break the question up into smaller pieces.

Then I adjust how much weight the different sources get in decision-making, as it differs for every situation. To make the final call on what to do with the data we have received and processed, we can take stock of where we obtain data and what we trust. For me, my body is the final call most of the time, but this isn't my natural inclination, and it takes effort. I do this because I've noticed, over years of paying attention, that my body is the source of data least affected by other people, especially compared with my mischievous mind, which has been heavily impacted by others. I've found that I am most happy with the decisions that I make based on what my body tells me. I believe my body integrates what my mind, heart, and spirit process and then arrives at its answers through a more profound analysis than I can understand. When in doubt, I bring my heart into focus, but I have intense and highly variable emotions that are often deeply hidden. Although they aren't untrue, they are all over the place, liable to change, and hard to find.

One common thread across survey responses is the simplicity of trustworthy data.

> "I have felt pulls on my solar plexus when information has come to me or before going into trance."
>
> —Laurie Pelham, medium

"Since I'm claircognizant, I sometimes just 'know' things without physical sensation. But other times, my body warns me (like a feeling of dread deep in the stomach) or a physical hesitation like a hand pushing me back and saying don't go in there. When I'm in a meditative space and receiving downloads or messages, I feel like I am in a trance and slightly floating outside my body and this plane."

—Shanta Ambady, artist, diviner, and channeler

"Simplicity. Whenever I receive a vision or a message that is 'right,' it is often instantaneous and matter-of-fact. The more complicated something is, the higher the possibility it is just my brain working overtime."

—John A. Rice, artist

"Their words, image, and voice are clear like loud thunder. There is no need or space for questioning."

—Haruka Aoki, artist and Earthling

DIVINATION

Finding an answer outside the mind (which uses reason) or the body (which offers intuition) is divination. Mediumship is a form of divination, as are tarot, *I Ching*, astrology, dreams, and runes. Anything can be made a divination by setting up a container in time and space, asking a question, and interpreting whatever appears in the container as the answer. For example, I will sometimes write a question on an index card, think about it before bed, place it under my pillow, and interpret whatever dreams I have that night as an answer to the question.

TRACKING DISCERNMENT

As you go about your day, start paying attention to all your decisions: when to eat, go to the bathroom, start or end a task, take a deep breath, pick up your phone, walk the dog, change the song, press on the brakes—the list is endless. You are making decisions almost every moment of the day.

As you become aware of how much your discernment engine is running, notice what effort you put out to make those decisions: Which ones do you think about? For which do you weigh options? Are some automatic?

Then focus on what information you use to make the decisions: the time on a clock, sensations in your body, brake lights in your eyes, the dog pawing at you.

After a few weeks of this, look back for patterns in the types of decisions you noticed, how you made those decisions, and on what type of information you tend to rely. Then you can experiment with adding or changing your sources. If you discover, for example, that the people around you tend to be the deciding factor—as in you eat when other people eat and you walk when other people walk—you may want to explore if there are times when you can use information from your feelings or the environment instead. If you find that your mind is mainly calling shots, like you go to the bathroom when you finish a paragraph rather than when your body says it's time (like me, right now, writing this), you might want to try listening more to your body and see what that shifts.

LEARNING FEELINGS

Come up with something you LOVE truly and deeply, without any reservation whatsoever. I use spaghetti, sequoia trees, the Mrs Eaves font, and other simple, nonemotional loves for this exercise. Find a safe, comfortable, low-sensory location to relax. Arrive in the space and quiet yourself, finding your focus in your heart or core. Say to yourself, "I LOVE [that thing you love]," and feel how your body responds. Then say to yourself, "I HATE [that thing you love]," and feel how your body responds. Note the difference and try it a few different times so you can start to learn how truth and lies sit in your body. Try it again with some basic statements of facts like 2 + 8 = 10 and "sugar is sweet" versus 2 + 8 = 15 and "sugar is sour."

Boundaries

To create a container and cultivate safety and connection, we need limits. Boundary setting happens internally and externally with our contacts and sitters. Prentis Hemphill, a therapist, somatics teacher and facilitator, political organizer, writer, and the founder of The Embodiment Institute, defines a boundary as "the distance at which I can love you and me simultaneously." Their definition hints at the importance and challenge of setting and maintaining boundaries.

To establish a baseline for working with the transphysical world, we can start by making explicit the many implied boundaries we follow daily. For example, consider how we approach strangers, what happens before speaking to someone, and how people initiate physical contact. We bring these unspoken protocols to our work in other domains to guide our actions and make requests to others.

In human relationships, we navigate highly specific boundaries, such as what topics we can broach over text or how long one person talks before another gets to speak. When working with other realms and beings, we may need to establish the most basic things, and it can be a challenge to remember to develop boundaries that most living humans know.

The practice of creating a container varies immensely across traditions. In Spiritualism, it is done verbally, inviting only those who come with intentions aligned with the mediums', for example, to promote healing and empowerment, as I learned at Fellowships. In the Native European and American practices I learned, we made physical circles around us to work in each time we connected, along with verbally acknowledging who and what is invited to connect. Each session and group needs its way of creating this container to protect participants.

I've established a few boundaries over the years in my mediumship practice. Not all are still in effect, but a few I reaffirm whenever I open a circle or read for a client. I offer these not as boundaries anyone else must maintain but as examples. Notice that I keep my agency by forming them as what I will do in reaction to my experience, rather than telling anyone else what to do. Write your own, starting with any that suit you from this list. As you work with your mediumship, keep expanding and changing your list. A good indicator that we need a boundary is when we find ourselves dropping out of connection, dysregulated, uncomfortable, or otherwise quickly changing state.

* **No living human contacts who aren't present:** I need explicit consent from all my contacts, and if the living person isn't with me to ask, I cannot connect with them.

* **No physical phenomena inside my house:** I need to feel safe at home. If I feel startled or scared at home by a spirit, I will close access to all spirits.
* **Do not pop in unannounced:** I need my personal space respected. I hold spirit office hours (Friday evenings, 7–9 p.m.) and respond only within those hours.
* **Make your intention known:** I need to ensure my safety and the safety of my sitters. I only work with contacts who share their intention with me and whose intention aligns with my own.
* **Speak to me in ways I can understand:** I need to be able to perceive the data a contact shares with me. If I receive indecipherable data, I will ask for it in another form, and if I still cannot understand, I will discard it.
* **Only those with information regarding the sitter's current life can contact me:** I need to provide useful information. I will discard messages that cannot be acted upon.
* **Only beings who come to support healing and empowerment can join a circle:** I need to keep my circle safe. If a spirit comes with information I feel could be harmful, I will ask them to phrase it in a way that will not be harmful, and if they cannot, I discard it.
* **Only identifiable relatives and friends can contact me:** I need to be able to identify my contacts in a reading. If I cannot, I will ask the sitter if they still want to hear the message before sharing it.
* **I do not look for specific contacts in a reading:** I need to respect the other realms. If a sitter insists on a particular person who does not join on their own accord, I will decline to give a reading.

I don't know how spirits and the unseen materialize, but I know that people can experience transphysical beings in the material world. If that's happening to you and you don't want it to, I'd suggest working with a *psychopomp* (a person who guides spirits) or someone specializing in materialization or clearings. The classic movie *The Sixth Sense* may have intended to scare viewers, but it was correct in suggesting to ask a bothersome spirit what they want as the first step in getting them to move on. I do the following when I get scared by something spooky and don't feel safe enough to have a conversation with the entity:

1. *Trust* that my body sensed something.
2. *Reaffirm* that I do not allow anything or anyone into my energy without my consent. With a strong exhale, I push out anyone else's energy, and with a strong inhale, I fill myself with my energy.
3. *Instruct* anything that might be around and scaring me to go back to where it came from.
4. *Recognize* that the most straightforward answer is often the right one.

This all applies to spirits or connections that are appearing within your nonphysical senses too. The processes and exercises in this book are meant to help those who are learning to turn on their abilities as much as those who want to turn them off. We need both skills. If you are not able to turn it (or another internal experience) off with these steps, regularly engaging in an engrossing activity that uses your mind, body, and spirit might help. Yard or housework, games or sports, and skilled activities that require focus do the trick for me. So does talking about it—refer back to your list of people who you can reach out to and make the call.

Contact Points

If I want to talk to the dead, I go where they are. I do not want to bring them *into* my body or mind; instead I want to make a container in which to meet them. The same is true for any other transphysical contact I work with. This is like the regular living world. We have rules about who can come into our homes (or, to push the point further, our physical bodies), under what circumstances, for how long, and how both parties must act during the visit.

It is possible to invite a contact into your physical being. This foundational principle of spirit and deity possession isn't part of this book because I've never done it. I don't leave out possession because it isn't possible—plenty of people practice it. My understanding is that possession is a form of mediumship where all or most of the mind and body are given over to a contact. For practitioners, the potential contacts are from a small and specific set of spirits and deities determined by their traditions. In other words, it is not any dead person, contact, or source. Possession is practiced usually within the context of religion, with and for the community, traditions, and beliefs that come along with it. If you feel called to learn about possession or believe it may happen to you without your consent, you can find experienced practitioners and teachers. An excellent place to look is the African diaspora religions and some pagan groups (although not all engage in the practice).

Likewise, I do not want to put myself *into* another being to make contact. As in regular life, we don't simply enter other people's homes or bodies. At first, we meet them somewhere neutral and convenient, shake hands, talk. Even if your contact exists in the corporeal world, you don't need to make your *contact point* inside their bodies. When I travel away from Coyo and want to connect with him, I imagine us both in a place that looks like the empty white space of the Construct in the movie *The Matrix*. When I want to connect with the dead, I move my attention to where I imagine the spirit realm—which is physically behind me.

Beyond

Contact points have two dimensions: what it is (the spirit realm, the Construct, Earth, creative consciousness) and where it is physically (behind me, above me, below me, in front of me, respectively). The physical place to which we move our attention ensures we do not invite anything into our body and changes the data we receive. How we visualize it sets up the space, preparing our meeting place for the conversation. Sometimes, when I move my attention to a contact point, I imagine myself and the contact I invited both there, like how I described Coyo in the Construct. Sometimes I put my focus in the place and notice what or who is around, which is how I work with the dead.

When I first learned mediumship, I started the connection by moving my attention to two o'clock, a foot and a half outside my head. From there, I accessed the spirit realm. Whatever I picked up while my attention was in that location, I shared with the sitter. How this place looked and how I accessed it changed with time. I started with a door I walked through. Then it was more like one of those round ship's windows. Later I would draw back a thick, velvet curtain. I did this for a few years until my teacher, Andrea Wadsworth, told me that the location I worked through was a tear in my energy field and that moving to directly above my head would be safer.

So I changed my process for connecting to the spirit realm. I couldn't use my visual metaphors anymore because things looked different in this new location, and even holding my attention above my head was shaky at first. I'd be distracted when I tried to put my attention there; I wanted to return to two o'clock. Intellectually, I knew that if I made a container and then put my attention into it, anything could be my access to the spirit realm, but it took me extra effort for months to focus like this. I trusted Andrea's assessment and felt that it made logical sense to work from there—it was central, and there was a natural point of attention, so I kept at it. I envisioned my energy in various ways—golden lines that I imagined smoothing was my favorite—to get comfortable with the twelve o'clock location.

Being a Responsible Medium

A year later, when a fellow student at Arthur Findlay, a Spiritualist college for learning mediumship outside London, suggested that spirit connects from behind us, I remembered that for years in my *tethering* practices I thought of the spirit realm as behind me because I can't see it and it is a mystery. I immediately took to this placement. In every reading I've done since, I have stuck with what feels most natural: I send my energy behind me and wait to see what I feel.

---

1. What are some contact points in your relationships with living humans? How does the physical place you meet a person change your interaction?

2. Where do you imagine your entrance to the spirit realm? What other realms, energies, or places would you like to connect with?

PART II

THE REASON(S) FOR MEDIUMSHIP

Welcome. Let me tell you a bit about yourself. You are different. You have tried, but something keeps you from reaching what you seek. This is a need for power. Like mediumship, power is not well understood in our culture. Power is *to do*. Martin Luther King, Jr., said, "Power, properly understood, is the ability to achieve purpose." We are beings; we are meant to be. However, we also need to do some doing, and for that we must use power. What we often cannot see from the vantage point of life today is that power is created together. King's quote continues, "One of the greatest problems of history is that the concepts of love and power are usually contrasted as polar opposites." Power is not ours to hold but something we cultivate, access, offer, and use through connection. We may think we can achieve independently, but nobody exists in isolation. I baked bread all by myself. Yes, this is an achievement for me. But it was possible because of an infinite thread of connected actions, people, and elements.

Our modern culture is built on abstracting time, resources, and energy into money and then taking, storing, and restricting access to that power. At one time, to bake bread, I needed to know where a patch of grains grew; later, I needed to be able to grow the grains or know someone who grew them. Now, usually, I need to have money to buy them. In this system, connection is devalued in favor of wealth. Mediumship, and all relating, is an act of resistance and healing for us because it puts our focus back on connection.

The Reason(s) for Mediumship

By expanding the web of connection, mediumship also breaks the socially agreed-upon, but far from universal, fixed opposition of life and death. Our current systems are predicated on such binary oppositions: spiritual/material, male/female, owners/workers, good/evil, crazy/sane, white/Black, rational/irrational. Life is much more blurry than our linguistic and social frameworks would lead us to believe. Binaries are convenient, but they are not real. Existence doesn't fit into little boxes. Breaking binaries changes our world by challenging hierarchies and limits.

To create a world that is different from what we currently experience, we need to be able to imagine something different. As Audre Lorde said, "The master's tools will never dismantle the master's house." Mediumship offers an engaging, and dare I say entertaining, way to practice envisioning what is not present in our physical environment.

These liberating features of mediumship contribute to making it taboo. It takes courage to step out of what is considered socially acceptable, especially if we already live at the margins of society. I don't know if I would have felt safe enough to become a medium if I hadn't found myself in Lily Dale, where it is considered normal. This book is meant to offer every reader a little respite from that social strain so that you too can cultivate a place where you feel safe to explore outside the bounds of the material world.

CHAPTER 4

NOT QUITE BORN AGAIN

Before moving to Lily Dale, I did try living in a rural place as an adult. A few years after I'd moved to Oakland, I struggled to get my consulting business going, and savings from my last full-time job had long run out, but my student loans and rent did not let up. A neighbor of my parents in Nevada City, California—a town in the Sierra Nevada foothills built around the 1849 gold rush and the site of my 2002 high school graduation—had a house for rent starting New Year's Day, 2015. I was already deep into fermenting kimchi, baking sourdough, and brewing kombucha; it was a natural step to move to the country, plant a large garden, get Nika a mate so we could have puppies, and find a weekly goat-milking gig.

Then, in the fall, I got a job offer at an e-commerce start-up in Manhattan. I was not excited to return to working for someone else, and I didn't want to move Nika and my pick of her litter, Coyo, to the city. I promised myself and the pups that once I paid off my student loans and had the money to buy a house, I'd quit my job and move back to the country for good. As it was, the constant financial stress of rent and loans did not pair well with the inconsistent nature of my independent consulting work, and I knew something needed to change. So I gave up that first rural idyll: I dusted off my power suits, traded my 1978 Mercedes 240D apocalypse machine for a practical 2009 Toyota Highlander, and my sister Amara and I drove us all to New York City.

Not Quite Born Again

Living in Crown Heights, Brooklyn, I saved like crazy, hardly participating in urban life, and paid off my debt in eighteen months. During that period, I went to my aunt's wedding, where I talked to my cousin Jamie Pfahl. At the time, Jamie was attending medical school in Colorado and taking care of our grandma's old cottage, which was a source of stress: Jamie could only get to Lily Dale rarely, and the house seemed to need endless repairs. She was considering giving up and letting it be reposessed. When she told me the annual taxes were around $1,200—less than one month of rent for me in Brooklyn—I immediately offered to take over the payments. A clear path to achieving what I'd set out to do had appeared. My loans were paid off. I could leave New York City and return to the country. Within a month, I was out of there.

My two-story cottage sits on a quarter-acre lot, flanked by a matching shed measuring 12 feet by 10 feet. It is located an hour south of Buffalo, enclosed in a gated, almost-150-year-old Spiritualist community on Cassadaga Lake. The Onöhsagwë:de' Cultural Center, which is owned and operated by the Seneca Nation of Indians, helped clarify that *Cassadaga* is believed to be a corrupted Seneca word pronounced "Gasdë:gö:h," which means "under the cliffs." The lake outlets to a creek of the same name, eventually ending up in the Mississippi. My neighbor Ray Taft, who was born in Lily Dale and whose grandfather was born on the Seneca Cattaraugus Territory nearby, says that the people who came to Cassadaga Lake in the second century were from around Cahokia and the urban lifestyle of the Midwest at that time. As someone who also came here to escape the city, I love this story.

My understanding is that the later history is less idyllic. Starting in the fifteenth century, the influx of Europeans, their diseases, and their attempts at assimilation strained all the Native Nations. The Erie or Wenro people likely inhabited Cassadaga Lake at that time. By the mid-1650s, widespread epidemics and conflict led both Nations to be dispersed and absorbed into Nations to the south or west. The majority were adopted into the Seneca.

In 1797, the Seneca Nation was forced to relinquish their rights to 3.25 million acres of their territory, including Cassadaga Lake. Thus, the land I now sit on arrived in European settlers' hands through duress, broken promises, and coercion, the details of which can be found in *The Collected Speeches of Sagoyewatha, or Red Jacket*, edited by Granville Ganter (Syracuse University Press, 2006). Despite generations of colonial imposition and unilateral policies enacted by the US government, the Seneca have maintained their strong culture and values in what is now called western New York. Visitors in the area can learn local history and culture at the Onöhsagwë:de' Cultural Center, and everyone can read about the Haudenosaunee and Seneca on their websites.

The wider western and central regions of New York, much of which is the traditional territory of the Haudenosaunee Confederacy (which includes the Seneca Nation and five others), developed into the "Burned-Over District." From the beginning of its settlement, it stood out as a hotbed of religious, social, and intellectual experimentation that has shaped American culture. In addition to Modern American Spiritualism, the area was home to numerous utopian communities, wide-ranging reform movements, Mormonism, Seventh-day Adventism, and the Shakers.

Even during the region's 1820s heyday brought on by the development of the Erie Canal, Cassadaga Lake sat surrounded by farmland. Public trance *demonstrations* came to the area in 1844, long after becoming popular in the Northeast. An extension of the railroad lines to the shores of Cassadaga Lake in 1870 facilitated the area's emergence on the Spiritualist scene. Spiritualist picnics had sprung up across the Northeast, where people gathered to hold lectures on philosophy and science, watch demonstrations, and practice mediumship in circles. These picnics gathered popularity and developed into week-long summer camps. With the nearby train stop, people from across the country could come to the new Lily Dale camp. By 1880, a group of Spiritualists calling themselves the Cassadaga Lake Free Association had purchased land and formally opened grounds dedicated to "Free Speech, Free Thought, and Free Investigation." By the 1890s, the camp was established essentially as it is found today, open for "camp season" all summer long, with restaurants, hotels, demonstrations, lectures, and classes. Anyone can visit during the season for a fifteen-dollar gate fee, but to live on the grounds is a much more involved process because Lily Dale is now a religious corporation—also known as a church.

I consider myself not to be a religious person. I was not raised in the religious tradition of my ancestors (or anyone else's) because my parents are functionally anti-religious. This departs from the generations before us on all sides, with long lines of Spiritualists (I'm the fifth generation in the Lily Dale cottage) and longer lines of Protestants and Catholics. As a kid, I occasionally went to all three churches with different grandparents. This gave me enough access to the mysteries of spirituality that, combined with my parents' rejection of religion, made it all deeply alluring to me.

This played itself out in my studies of scientific frontiers and dabbling in esoterica before my shock at landing in the religious community of Lily Dale. I moved here as an economic decision, although curiosity and the quiet offered by a rural lifestyle also factored in. I had not considered any religious aspect. However, relocating to Lily Dale involved more than packing up and moving in. It was a three-year-long process, requiring me to adopt the religion of Spiritualism formally by joining a church, hiring two lawyers, finding three community members to vouch for me, signing a form that included confirming I am a Spiritualist, and going before the Lily Dale Assembly board of directors (most of whom are practicing, if not professional, psychics).

Regardless, this was much easier for me than paying rent in New York City. I quickly began learning mediumship, but it wasn't until I started researching the history of the current Spiritualist religion as the early Spiritualist Movement that I became emotionally and intellectually tied to it. I'm uneasy calling myself a Spiritualist to outsiders, but within the gates, many of my neighbors and I consider it a lifestyle rather than a religion. Religion aside, the Spiritualist

Movement gives me depth and takes mediumship closer to the sacred because it is a tale of resistance. The fact that the last modern revival of mediumship in the United States supported some of the folks leading multiple social change movements still gives me goosebumps—and hope. There is something more here than our individual development and a compelling diversion.

Mediumship fascinates me; it is a forgotten birthright I want to bring back for myself and others. It has helped me heal and expand myself, mainly by allowing me to explore and confront what is not conscious or rational. At the collective level, mediumship can do the same thing. This capacity makes it a powerful tool without inherent polarity but capable of bringing both good and bad, as we will see in this quick look at Modern American Spiritualism's history.

Modern American Spiritualism

Humans have always maintained relationships with their dead. How could we not? They are us. But we have always been separate from our dead and needed to develop explanations, practices, and tools to make contact. Every group of people, however large or small, at any time and place, will have such methods, some of which could fall into our working definition of mediumship. Some would be considered far more advanced and established than what I am presenting in this book, as it represents one recent and limited manifestation of an ancient and global phenomenon. I appreciate how humans in one corner of the world, a few generations after eliminating most tools for connecting with the dead, collected and redeveloped methods and shared them among themselves.

Much is written on this specific Spiritualism, including its causes, impacts, and histories with stories of heroes and villains. I explored it in a Spiritualist reading group I started through Morbid Anatomy, an organization working at the intersection of death and culture, and in the Lily Dale Museum with Ron Nagy, Lily Dale's historian. I also learned a great deal from Charvonne Carlson, a national Spiritualist teacher, commissioned healer, certified medium, and director of the Church of Peace, whose exceptional understanding of the history and generous support helped me see the bigger picture.

Throughout the book, I often call this Modern American Spiritualism simply Spiritualism. The word *spiritualism* refers to a belief in the spiritual, as opposed to restricting existence to the material. In this sense, it applies to spirituality in general. However, capital-S Spiritualism developed into a religion in the United States and is a specific form distinct in its history, beliefs, and practices.

Spiritualism cultivated not only the practice of talking to the dead but a foundation in science and philosophy. Drawing from the cultural upheavals of abolition, the labor movement, women's rights, and many others during the mid-to-late 1800s, Spiritualism thrived by blending new ideas. Mediumship, in the particular form emerging as Spiritualism, practically exploded into the culture of western New York in the late 1840s. It may seem surprising that a movement so focused on talking to the dead could be widely popular in the United States, but in *The Other World: Spiritualism and Psychical Research in England, 1850–1914* (Cambridge: Cambridge University Press, 1985), Janet Oppenheim says that Spiritualists' "concerns and aspirations placed them—far from the lunatic fringe of their society—squarely amidst the cultural, intellectual, and emotional moods of the era." We see the threads of the early Spiritualist tradition woven into many later groups, from Theosophy, Black Spiritual Churches, and New Age to the formal, Internal Revenue Service–recognized religion of Lily Dale.

Spiritualism is something of a religious add-on; it doesn't require conversion. The Spiritualist belief structure fits within most religions and isn't egregious to non-religious or counter-religious folks either. It doesn't have a creation myth or a foundational text. There is no leader or governing body, and there are no rituals or requirements. Although Spiritualism has no singular claim to the practice of mediumship, it gave me my first understanding of the practice. Before Spiritualism, I studied shamanism, *I Ching*, tarot, transcendental meditation, and Buddhism. Nothing has opened me up to a spiritual life like Spiritualism has, and with my locational and ancestral (although not by blood) relationships to it, I feel in a place to share it with others.

Early Ties with Abolition

The oft-told story of the advent of Spiritualism begins with the Fox sisters, a pair of adolescent girls who began to communicate with a spirit via knocking sounds in their home outside Rochester, New York, in 1848. Usually left out of that story is Amy and Isaac Post's role in the Fox sisters' and Spiritualism's emergence into the cultural mainstream. It has been richly documented by Nancy A. Hewitt in *Radical Friend* (The University of North Carolina Press, 2018).

Amy and Isaac were both born into Quaker families on Long Island, New York, around the turn of the nineteenth century. Quakers—who subscribe to a Christian religion founded by George Fox, unrelated to the Fox sisters, who were Methodists—are generally known for their pacifism and commitment to reform. By the 1820s, the Posts shifted into a splinter group of more radical Quakers called Hicksites, led by Amy's cousin. The Hicksites grew out of two Long Island groups of Quakers who had manumitted the people they enslaved and committed themselves to abolition in the 1770s. In the 1830s, Hicksites, including the Posts, worked with the Seneca people to support the fight to keep their remaining lands. They had strong views on the rights of all people to live with freedom and respect.

By the time the Fox sisters first heard their rappings, the Posts had moved to Rochester, founded the Western New York Anti-Slavery Society, and become leaders of abolitionist activities in the area. Their home was an oft-used stop on the Underground Railroad. It also served as a meeting point for many of those we now associate with abolition—Frederick Douglass, William Lloyd Garrison, and Sojourner Truth—and the Fox sisters. Although many people contributed to the growth of Spiritualism, those who came across it through the Posts were among the most celebrated and credible, both then and now.

The Posts included both Black and white individuals in their social and activist circles. This was extremely uncommon at the time, even for abolitionists. A generation after the Posts died, most Americans continued to lead segregated private and religious lives, while public segregation didn't legally come to an end until the Civil Rights Act of 1964.

A Foundation of Individual Responsibility

Having been to a Quaker meeting and many Spiritualist circles, I see how much Spiritualism's development owes to this early comingling. A Quaker meeting today still involves all attendees sitting quietly, waiting for inspiration from the Holy Spirit, and then standing to share it with the group. We do the same to learn mediumship, albeit with a different contact. I do not think Spiritualism would have developed without introducing this format, along with the technical skills of connecting to spirit honed by the Quakers.

The foundational belief that makes Quakerism (and later, Spiritualism) different from other Christian religions is that everyone has permission—and the ability—to connect directly with the divine. The emerging concepts of personal responsibility and personal freedoms were defining features of culture in the United States at the time when Spiritualism emerged. This contributed to the appeal of Spiritualism, and there is overlap between the people fighting for individual liberties and those practicing Spiritualism.

In *Determined Spirits: Eugenics, Heredity and Racial Regeneration in Anglo-American Spiritualist Writing, 1848–1930* (Edinburgh University Press, 2012), Christine Ferguson shows that some spiritualists, instead of explaining the phenomenon of mediumship as a capacity everyone has, understood it as a result of destiny, specifically genetic inheritance. This line of thinking leaves no room for change through effort, experience, or the impact of society. There is a slippery slope from this type of individual exceptionalism into ableism, hereditary determinism, a rejection of free will, and eugenics. The writings of prominent Spiritualists such as Andrew Jackson Davis and Paschel Beverly Randolph show that some Spiritualists fell into this trap while paradoxically arguing for progressive reform. The inability to see and accept difference and collective responsibility can move even the most earnest desire to improve people's lives into dangerous territory.

A Women-Led Movement

From its earliest days to today, Spiritualism has been led by women and offered women a place and a voice they had yet to access in the United States. Anne Braude's work, in particular *Radical Spirits* (Beacon Press, 1989), has beautifully articulated this relationship between early Spiritualism and feminism. The Posts, especially Amy, were also involved in the early women's rights movement. This movement did not start with a focus on gaining the vote, as many early leaders were Quakers and not involved in "worldly" activities like politics. The early focus included women gaining the rights to own and control property and earnings, autonomy over their bodies (including wearing pants, leaving marriages, and choosing whether or not to bear children), the right to education, and a general push to have access to life outside the home.

While today most professional mediums focus on individual message work, in the early days, collective mediumship in the form of trance lectures, sittings, and circles were fashionable. At the time, the most famous mediums were women, and there were very few public places where they were allowed to do their work. Women gathering to organize for their rights had similar issues, and Spiritualist groups helped increase the number of people advocating for women to speak in public. Black Methodist churches, Quaker meeting places, and theaters were some of the early locations that allowed women on the podium both to demonstrate mediumship and work toward gender equality.

Spiritual but not Religious

One of the most significant appeals of early Spiritualism was that it offered people a way to experience spirituality without religion. While we are familiar with this concept today, there were few socially acceptable examples in the mid nineteenth century. Those available, such as transcendentalism and freemasonry, were limited by intellectual barriers and an explicit restriction to white men, respectively. After Christianity's shift away from relationships with the dead in the Reformation, which Erik R. Seeman details in *Speaking to the Dead in Early America* (University of Pennsylvania Press, 2019), many Protestants sought a more open approach to relationships with the dead. The personal and philosophical implications of contacting the dead, combined with a commitment to shifting the dominant social hierarchy, made Spiritualism attractive to many.

The phenomenon of white Christians exploring new forms of religious expression that flourished in the Burned-Over District—leading to Spiritualism and numerous other sects—was deeply influenced by the area's Haudenosaunee community and people of African descent. Diverse spiritual beliefs demonstrating greater openness toward spirituality offered new perspectives on spirits and the afterlife, helping to broaden many would-be Spiritualists' minds. For example, the Posts spent time with both groups through their work on the Joint Committee on Indian Affairs and the Western New York Anti-Slavery Society, as fellow community members and neighbors, and within lifelong friendships. Influence also took place at a broader level, as cultures organically mixed and developed in the area.

Spiritualism, then, served as a vehicle for ideas from Native, Black, and, later, Eastern spirituality to work their way into white culture. Much of this is textbook cultural appropriation, as the adoption often happened without permission, acknowledgment of the source, or even, until many years after Spiritualism's emergence, tolerance for the original practitioners. I am hopeful for the future as perspectives change to recognize these cultural debts.

A Shift from Social Justice to Social Respectability

As a rejection of church hierarchy and dogma, Spiritualism offered many people a sincere and novel form of spiritual practice and community. In addition to providing the solace of direct connection with dead loved ones, the philosophy surrounding this capacity hinted at a broad-based theology formulated primarily on the continuation of life after death. It began as a fiercely independent community of people practicing informally in their homes and small groups, and it quickly grew into a mature system of sharing beliefs through circles, lectures, pamphlets, and newspapers. The early history of Spiritualism is well-documented through these channels. Still, neither the government nor law considered it a legitimate religion because it lacked formal religious organization.

I got a deeper understanding of Spiritualism's respectability politics from Ericka White Dyson's "Spiritualism and Crime: Negotiating Prophecy and Police Power at the Turn of the Twentieth Century" (UMI, 2010). She explains that vague vagrancy and anti-fortune-telling laws have long been questionable ways to police the behavior of primarily marginalized people in the Western world. As white, middle-class Spiritualists in the late 1800s working as mediums were increasingly arrested under these laws, Spiritualists took the stance that they were being arrested for practicing their religion, which is in opposition to the legal right to freedom of religion in the United States.

After at least twenty years of efforts to organize, Spiritualists finally joined in 1893 to create the National Spiritualist Association, largely to support this stance on freedom of religion. Now called the National Spiritualist Association of Churches (NSAC), whose member churches require mediums to go through formal ordination procedures. The creation of clergy is somewhat antithetical to the original doctrine and professed beliefs of Spiritualists, a story of respectability politics grown to protect mediums' ability to practice legally and to charge for their work.

Regressive Movements and Spiritual Bypassing

While the Posts were proud "universalists"—a precursor to intersectional feminism—in time, the women's rights movement evolved into the suffrage movement. Rather than finding strength with multiple causes, they splintered over which should take precedence: rights for women or rights for Black men.

Black Americans adopted and contributed to Spiritualism from its earliest days, at least partly because of its affinity with traditional African religions and relatively egalitarian structure that rejected the racialized caste system operating in the broader society during that time. However, once the Spiritualist movement had calcified into the Spiritualist religion, the National Spiritualist Association (NSA) showed itself to be decidedly not progressive. Rather than fight against the existing racism of American society, the NSA succumbed to the prevalent mindset of the times, organizing its Black members into segregated auxiliary organizations. Then, in the mid-1920s, the (white) leadership removed all the Black members. This split Spiritualism in the United States and fueled the Black Spiritual Movement and the National Colored Spiritualist Association of Churches. It also left a white Spiritualism that has yet to recover from the loss of an entire community of like-minded people.

Plenty of close-minded activity still sits alongside mediumship and Spiritualism. Some stems from the same desire for certainty that produces conservatism in any other realm of society. More comes from the tendency to skip over the hard parts of life or explain them away with platitudes rather than working through them. I include these realities not to vilify or absolve Spiritualism or Spiritualists but to open up about our history and elucidate our context. I want to be clear that while talking to the dead is a radical act, it doesn't automatically make a person open-minded. No spiritual, religious, philosophical, scientific, or otherwise label-based identification is enough to put a person on moral high ground.

1. What is your spiritual and religious history? How have you followed, rejected, or expanded the beliefs you've been exposed to so far?

2. What religious and spiritual traditions and practices are interesting to you? How did you come across them? How have you engaged with their tools, ideas, or practitioners?

3. What is your understanding of personal and collective responsibility? How have religion and spirituality influenced it?

4. How has your and your family's racial and class identity influenced your spiritual and religious beliefs and your ability to practice them? How about other aspects of your identity? How have these identities affected your feelings about and engagement with social justice and spiritual bypassing?

CHAPTER 5

HEALING THROUGH CONNECTION

I've moved often, but usually for work or school, so I had a built-in social scene upon arrival. The move to Lily Dale wasn't simply shifting from urban to rural life, secular to religious life, and office to work-from-home life. I went from the biggest city in America, with an average age of thirty-eight years old and 23 percent of the population over age sixty-five, to a community of fewer than two hundred people, with an average age of sixty-eight and 69 percent of the people over the age sixty-five. To say I didn't fit in is an understatement.

I slowly got to know my neighbors, convinced them to invite me to their card games, offered to help them with their websites, begrudgingly reopened a Facebook account, and enthusiastically attended many, many luncheons. Still, by the time the pandemic hit, I felt like I'd already been isolating for two years.

As a practice of connection, mediumship took me through a loneliness renaissance. It helped me shift my understanding of relating, how I dealt with disconnection, the tools I had to remedy loss and loneliness, and ultimately turned me into a not-lonely person. I am more solitary than ever, but my relationships are deeper, broader, stronger, and more impactful than before. This is because I expanded whom I considered for a relationship and then made better connections with those I had found available. But first I had to learn why I felt lonely and why it impacted me so much.

I had to consider that perhaps I am lonely because I haven't tried hard enough, am unlikeable, or am not good at relating to people. I read studies on loneliness, ran a survey online with my far-away friends, wrote about it, and graphed how lonely I had been on average each year. I realized that loneliness is largely a function of time and place and that I am not alone in feeling alone. In 2023, the US Surgeon General released an epidemic advisory unrelated to COVID-19. This was an advisory for loneliness and isolation built from decades of research across a half dozen scientific disciplines, so it didn't even directly refer to the crisis point reached during the pandemic. The advisory shares that half of our population reported feeling lonely and that rates are highest among young adults. Critically, this degree of loneliness represents an "urgent public health concern.... In order to promote health, change is needed across the full scope of the social-ecological model."

Aggregating data across 148 studies, scientists showed that social connection was an independent risk factor for all causes of mortality. More than lifestyle choices (like drinking and smoking), clinical risk factors (such as high blood pressure or cholesterol levels), environmental factors (like pollution), or medical interventions (for example, vaccines, medications, rehabilitation), loneliness, isolation, and social connection influence our health.

As an inherently social activity, mediumship is a tool for our loneliness toolbox, and working on reducing loneliness is a tool for our health-care toolbox. Managing social connection involves almost our entire lives. Nearly every aspect of who we are and how we live influences the potential for—and our ability to—connect with others. From our health and mobility to our family structure to the amount of outdoor space and methods of transport available, our social lives are constructed out of the building blocks of our daily experience. The dead offer an extension of our lives—one limited almost exclusively by social norms. Once we get past the barrier of thinking it is okay or not, we don't have to go anywhere, buy anything, or feel any particular way to connect with the dead.

Relating

One reason we consider only living people to be potential sources of relationships is that language feels like our only way to communicate. The tools of mediumship open the possibility of communication with not only the dead but anything else you might want to talk to. Before we start practicing mediumship, we'll take some time to consider who and what we might want to include in our network of potential contacts.

Mediumship doesn't need to come at the expense of relationships with living humans. It is an opportunity for us to explore, be our best or worst selves, practice changes we want to make, and learn what it means to be in relationship.

When we develop relationships, we open the possibility of working together or *cocreating*. It is easy to see this with a musical instrument or a house. We understand why we'd do that with a living person—we don't walk around demanding things from people (hopefully). We need to get to know them to learn what they desire, can do, and are willing to do. I suggest we do the same with other types of beings and through relationships in other realms.

The receptivity we learn with mediumship contrasts with the ways we often interact with others. Sociologists studying our culture's current lack of relating distill it into three key defining traits of a modern life rooted in colonialism: mobility, consumption, and the fragmentation of social bonds. Being able (or forced) to move around significantly reduces the likelihood of proximity to people we know or a place we have ties to. Consumption has fueled the constant changes in our environment as cities grow and rural areas shift from forests and fields to strip malls and housing tracts. When we lose the places and people we know, we must build new relationships, which takes time, risk, and energy.

I see a habit of interaction as transaction in our culture—and myself. Nobody wants to admit they talk to you mostly because they need something. This is profoundly different from what I experienced in other parts of the world I visited for work, particularly Kenya and Uganda. It annoyed me at first. Everything felt like it took so long because everyone had to talk to everyone else all the time. *Come on, come on, let's go*, I'd think. My colleagues would pat my shoulder and smile. They knew this three-fold warp of colonization conditioned me; no studies needed to prove it. They knew I only interacted with people who could give me something. Pat, pat. I can't believe they didn't hate me—I would have if I'd realized the truth of my motives wasn't about being on time. I see now what they might have then: poor, lonely, hurried white lady. No family. No roots. No time to chat.

Social connection is made up of structure, function, and quality. What I witnessed around me in East Africa was a drastic expansion of how I handled social connection. Although my experience was limited to a few months over several years, I was engaged in design research on each trip. Most of my time was spent talking to people, being passed through their social networks, and joining them in their daily lives to learn about their experiences.

I discovered that the people I met there generally knew way more people and had more regular social interaction than those I know in the United States—simply, the social structures were larger. People had more inclination to support each other, and there wasn't an expectation that each person would do everything for themselves. People helped each other where they could, creating connections with a high degree of function. From my outsider's vantage point, relationships seemed to have a positive quality, even in the face of poverty, which I'd been taught was to be avoided at all costs. Now I understand that, at least for me, isolation is worse.

Note that there can be downsides to very close communities in the form of the perceived (and actual) need to conform. I was indirectly researching relationship quality for some of my time there, with a project investigating how to support people who are HIV positive, and I did witness the adverse effects of tight-knit communities in the form of exclusion and bias. So, of course, there is never a perfect answer. We humans always have our struggles.

NOTICING THE BODY

Throughout the book, you will find guided meditations like the one following. You can access recordings for all of them on the Normalize Talking to the Dead website.

Please note these meditations focus on being present in the body, breathwork, and *attentional travel*. They may only be comfortable and effective for some. You can stop anytime and return to ordinary reality in your physical space. If you come across a section that doesn't feel right for you, ignore the instruction or make up your own that is better suited for your experience. The goal of this meditation is to help you spend time noticing the body.

Start by settling into your breath. Allow your attention to move from there into your toes. Far, far away from your mind, eyes, and ears, to where the only sense is temperature and pressure. How the skin feels. What can those toes pick up? Can they feel the temperature of the room? Do they know what surrounds them? What's underneath them, what's above them? Are they able to listen? Or see in their own way? If you could move your eyes to your toes, what would be in your line of vision? What could you hear from that perspective? What could you smell?

Move up your legs and torso to the middle of your chest alongside your heart. We feel emotion there; we can feel the pressure of our heartbeat. We can listen to the sound of blood rushing through the ventricles, coursing around our bodies. If we sit here momentarily and imagine we have eyes on this part of our body, what can we see from this perspective? What does the front of the room look like at your heart level? And turning those eyes around, what's behind you? If you had ears on the front and the back of your chest, would you hear differently from the ears on the left and right side of your head?

Leave your heart behind and move up through your neck and into your brain, into the middle of your head. Where the two sides of your brain come together is a little highway. If you sit here, you can hear both sides of your mind. This spot, neutral in your head, has nothing coming from it. But you can watch things moving between the left and right hemispheres.

Hold your next inhale, move your attention to the left side of your brain, and allow your head to tilt simultaneously. So, in one motion, breathe in, tilt your head to the left, move your attention to the left side of your head, and feel. Focus on the left half of your brain, simply noticing that place.

When you next breathe in, bring your head back to neutral. Exhale there and on the next inhale, move your attention and slightly tilt your head to the right, feeling what's in that side of your brain, simply noticing what it feels like being there for a moment.

And on your next inhale, bring your attention back to the middle of your head. Bring your head straight, going back to a neutral position. Exhale. Now, on your next inhale, allow your attention to move down to the back of your head, right above where it meets the neck. This is the reptilian brain, the oldest part of it. Notice what it feels like there.

On your next inhale, allow your attention to move back to the middle of your brain. Exhale. When you breathe in, shift your focus to just inside your forehead. The newest part of the brain is one that many other species do not have. See what it feels like there. Now, take a step outside your skull and move your attention a little bit beyond your forehead, just on the other side of your skin. Then, move back to right behind your eyes, prepare to open them, and return to your physical space.

Cocreation

Mediumship does happen in long-standing and effective contexts where the human commands, conjures, or otherwise dictates what contacts do. I learned another approach. My first teacher, Marza, taught me her medicine ways, a blend of teachings and practices based on her Ojibwe and Celtic lineage, and her lifelong work with the Yavapai and many Native people worldwide. She showed me that all our experiences on this planet can be seen as cocreation, that we are never truly in isolation, and it is a loss—a mistake—to act as if we are.

This understanding blended seamlessly with my nascent Spiritualist mediumship work, giving me a safe, less extractive, and more sustainable foundation. Connection is better built on love than reliant on control. I now perceive relationships with everything, and it feels right for me. My house, the food I eat, the ground I walk on, the cards I use, the art materials I have... I could go on forever. I relish the opportunity to make everything and anything a potential partner in life, for whatever task or time, large or small. This cocreation, or relating, involves cultivating the following:

* **Empathy:** Develop lines of communication that work for each contact.
* **Curiosity:** Ask questions and give focus to the other.
* **Expression:** Share my intentions, desires, and thoughts.
* **Reciprocity:** Acknowledge and provide a respectful exchange.

If we are to be a medium—that is, an agent of the in-between—we are asking for input from someone else. What we want, need, feel, or think aren't the only things that matter. Relating reminds us of this part of the process and brings us to a place of curiosity and care for the other.

It takes time for an adult new to this idea to learn to respect nonliving things, the trappings of our minds, and the plants and animals around us. I learned this by having pets and awakening to discomfort with being their "owner." When Nika first came into my life, I started with training to communicate what I wanted her to do. Empathy dawned on me, bringing a constant awareness of what it would be like to be her. Then I started to see how her biological needs were often at odds with my desires and conveniences. So much of our relationships with pets, when dictated by cultural expectations rather than in-the-moment realities, center on control and our comfort. To relate with animals, we need to step outside domination. I sometimes get embarrassed when I walk Coyo on a leash and wild animals see us. Outside the confines of human expectation, including strict leash laws, it is cruel to restrain a being by a rope attached to its neck. To combat my barbarism, I agree with Coyo that I'll find us wild places he can run around a few times a week and as many other ways I can offer him freedom to listen to his own desires.

The Crisis of Connection

Looking back, one of the reasons I learned to disconnect from my body and those around me was that, so often, connection brings pain—not only in the form of direct harm but also through the experience of watching another be harmed. As I've developed my connection capacities, I sometimes feel overwhelmed by the harm and trauma happening around me. I feel pain at every animal lying dead on the side of the road. Every time I witness an adult treating a child callously. I'm overwhelmed with emotion the moment I connect with my heart. I have not found an answer to this sensitivity. It comes with the territory and requires patience, attention, support, and acceptance to continue. On some days it is too much, and I withdraw. This world is full of suffering—but it is also full of hope, love, and beauty. Opening to the former gives us access and the ability to see the latter, but it takes effort to keep that focus balanced.

Embodiment

Shifting focus from the mind to the body has been a fascinating step in balancing these two aspects of my experience. Noticing what is happening in my body as I am living has expanded my available data on the world around me and my responses to it. It has helped me know myself better. This has been a long-term, ongoing project that I anticipate engaging in as long as I have a body. Then there is the moment-to-moment experience of "being present" in my body. This is not always accessible to me; when it isn't, I cannot force it. When I can get fully present with my body, it is as if my spirit falls into my core, and I physically feel its weight.

Modern Spiritualist mediumship is often referred to as "mental" mediumship. This is intended to juxtapose "physical" mediumship because the phenomena brought through take the form of words rather than anything tangible or externally perceived, like *ectoplasm*, rappings, moving furniture, etc. This distinction is misleading to me because my mediumship experience begins and ends in my body. My mind is the last place I want to be, as I am intentionally not thinking. My mind may be the processing and output center, but I receive data through my body, so I use *embodied mediumship* for the practices outlined in this book.

In my survey, I asked what embodiment meant and learned that, for nearly all respondents, the body plays a starring role in their practice. Most people use more than one of the following, but the body is generally the primary tool for shifting awareness to prepare for connection.

Embodied presence: Practitioners recognize the importance of being fully present in our bodies to access our psychic abilities effectively.

Physical sensations: Noticing specific bodily sensations informs us as we connect; common examples are tingling, pressure, warmth, or changes in breathing patterns.

Grounding and centering: Moving from regular awareness to body awareness to create a receptive state can be initiated through grounding and centering focus on the earth or body.

Energetic awareness: Changing the scope of attention, such as extending to surrounding energy fields or narrowing to a cellular level within the body, helps to shift awareness.

Body as an antenna: The body can be viewed as a receptor for psychic information, with different body parts acting as "antennae" for receiving messages or sensations.

Somatic empathy: The body can physically feel sensations corresponding to the experiences of our contacts.

Movement: Bodily movement like walking, dancing, or gesturing can channel energy or express messages.

Body posture: Some practitioners find that specific body positions or gestures help facilitate their connection to spirit or intuitive information.

Breathwork: Conscious breathing allows us to actively enter altered states or enhance focus.

Healing practices: Incorporating bodywork or energy healing techniques are tangible applications for psychic connection.

The Senses

In mediumship, setting up a quiet space and presence is all in service of listening. We exist materially, with birds chirping, cars driving, fridges humming, and fans whirring. Listening, in mediumship, is more than sounds and ears. We're learning to listen with our entire body. And we're moving from listening to the external world to hearing our internal world.

We understand that our senses encompass our entire connection with the outside world. We experience what our ears, eyes, noses, skin, and tongue capture and our brain processes. We sense, or experience, input through our body—and we perceive, or use, that information.

Before moving away from the corporeal world, I must tell you that we have three more senses than we're commonly taught. These are proprioception, balance, and interoception.

Proprioception tracks all our body parts and gives us a sense of where the body ends. It involves sense organs in the muscles, joints, and nerves.

The *vestibular*, or balance, system senses our equilibrium and movement so that we know where we are in space. It is a group of tiny organs in the ear.

Interoception is how we monitor bodily sensations, allowing us to notice what happens inside us. It includes our ability to feel our organs, heartbeat, breath, pain, hunger and other digestive activities, and temperature. Interoception is intimately tied to our ability to discern our emotions.

All emotions start with physiological changes in the body, whether we notice these shifts or not. So, as we develop our ability to feel our body reacting to the world, we can detect oncoming emotions earlier and more accurately. These three senses bridge us from the outside world to the internal world, where mediumship happens.

The Self and Body

In any state or form, the body is a miraculous thing. The body fails, however, to be a safe or comfortable place for many of us. In an interview, Dr. Stephen Porges, who developed the polyvagal theory, said, "I think the whole issue [of the success of an individual] can be reduced to [a] metaphor in which we estimate the degree in which we live inside our body or outside our body, whether we witness ourselves or respect ourselves, or whether we are subservient to the explicit world and the defining features of everything around us. It's not that one strategy is right and the other is wrong, or one is good and the other bad. It's that there is a dance between the two."

NOTICING THE SENSES

We see endless variations in how sensation and perception work within our species and all living things. Think about, notice, or research other ways of experiencing the world. Dogs have more than five times as many olfactory receptors than we do. Pigeons see a different spectrum of light than humans. While sunshine on my skin can feel anywhere from life-giving to life-threatening, with the nature of photosynthesis, I can imagine that light on leaves feels very different to a tree.

When we lose the ability to use one sense, the body often gives more space to another, letting it take up more brainpower to give it more robust capacities. If one of your senses is impaired, this exercise allows us to catch up with you. Most of us who have full faculty of all our senses take them for granted, and we need a moment to acknowledge that our capacity for sensing is fluid and depends not only on our physical ability but also on our attention to the senses.

Consider how much of your day relies on your eyes. If you've ever had a problem with your eyes or if you wear corrective lenses, what happens when you don't have as much access to vision? Another way to assess how much we depend on sight is to check what your hands feel. Once you've assessed, take a quick moment to close your eyes and feel your hands again. Try it with hearing, too—what sounds do you hear? How does it change your perception if you close your eyes and listen?

As you go through your day, notice when your senses are bringing you information and how it affects you. Which senses do you feel comfortable with? Which senses are more often a source of pain or frustration? For example, I have an especially acute sense of smell. Right now, it is spring, which for me is the season when the world begins to smell again. Walking down the street or through the woods, I enjoy the delights of all the plants and everything in the soil coming back alive with warmth and water. I also have nightmarish memories of toilets around the world. When I lost my sense of smell with COVID-19, I realized I couldn't tell what food was safe to eat out of my fridge. I have since stopped keeping such old leftovers, but it was a hard habit to break, and without the experience, I might not have noticed how much I rely on my nose.

Try switching senses out for one another—this is about getting in tune with our instrument, whatever we have. There is no specific sense used for mediumship, but we all have those we prefer. Imagine seeing a feeling, tasting a sound, or hearing an image. This is called *synesthesia*, and some people are born with senses that cross over like this. Even if we don't have synesthesia, we can imagine it and use the concept to deepen our relationship with our senses.

Imagine sitting before a piece of fruit. Spend time trying each sense to notice what it offers—imagine its taste, smell, feel, and sound; close your eyes and see it. Try it again with the actual fruit and see what your physical senses add to your awareness. Go back to imagining and notice if and how memory alters your experience.

We were required to study both mediumship and spiritual healing in the Fellowships of the Spirit program. In Modern American Spiritualism, the laying on of hands is included in every church service, typically before mediumship demonstrations. I felt like this was an odd inclusion in services, having no obvious tie to the philosophy of Spiritualism, and I lamented having to study it at Fellowships. Alongside our classes on mediumship, we were required to take hands-on healing classes and needed to complete as many documented healings per year (seventy!) as readings.

To my surprise, the hours and hours we spent noticing every tiny bodily sensation strengthened my interoception and proprioception. I slowly learned how to spend time in my body and notice its experiences, which became the foundation of my mediumship practice.

Although they can appear similar to one another, sensations are emergent phenomena based on our external environment interacting with our internal physiology, so they are truly unique. Each blush, every rumble, is its own. Sensations can occur anywhere in individual elements (organs, muscles, bones), systems (the skin, digestive tract), parts of the body (hands, legs), and across the entire being. Sensations have depth, size, texture, sound, movement, shape, and time. Here are a few examples from respondents to my survey.

> "Usually, my tummy gurgles when I am fully aware."
> —Carrie Everett, animal communicator, Reiki Master, evidential medium

> "I can sense my skin's outside. My whole body is able to receive."
> —Theresa R., medium and tarotist

> "When I begin to feel present, my awareness directs itself inward to me and my body. I begin to feel as if all my cells are spreading outward at once, and the spaces between are becoming activated and given equal value in my sensory awareness."
> —Kathleen Boldt, spiritual medium

Healing through Connection

"It feels like everything is slowing down, and it seems like I can feel every cell. It is quiet and calm."

—Susan Doyle, medium

"It begins with a cool wave that travels from the base of my spine up to my mid-back and spreads through my chest. I feel a quality of warmth bloom from the mid-body to the limbs and edges."

—Mikella Millen, energy work and trance work practitioner

---

1. The body takes food and turns it into more of itself. What else does your body do that you barely notice? What if other things could do what your body does—like if a computer could heal itself or a bed could sense you were near it and pull back the covers for you? Even in nature, the human body stands out as exceptional. What if cats could move in unison to a rhythm? What if an owl could learn to sing like a sparrow?

2. Pain is an especially loud signal from the body. How do you react to pain? What did you do the last time something hurt, physically or emotionally?

DEVELOPING CONNECTION TO THE BODY

Are you familiar with how it feels to become present with your body? I frequently do this over the course of a day or even a mediumship session. Yet there are many times when I cannot feel that presence. In those moments, I look for any sensation I can feel within the body. That may only be where I am touching another object, and even that feeling may dissipate when I try to focus on it. Here are a few exercises to learn and explore developing embodiment skills.

You can start right now: Close your eyes—what can you feel? Your skin on a surface? The temperature in the room? Your weight on which points and at what intensity? Make a daily practice of periodically noting what is happening with your body, where it ends, and where sensations occur.

Try hands-on healing: Find someone with whom you both feel safe enough to put your hands right above or gently resting on the other person's shoulders. Set a timer for a few minutes, no more than fifteen. As the sitter, do your best to keep your attention within your body, following the sensations, feelings, and thoughts that arise. As the healer, ask the sitter if you may work with their body and energies. If you receive a yes, place your hands. Later you can explore working with various contacts, but start by asking to connect to a safe source of healing energy outside your body, such as the earth, the sun, or the God of your understanding. When you establish that connection, healing energy from your contact will flow into yourself, then through your hands into your sitter. When the timer goes off, take a moment to thank your contact and sitter, then withdraw your attention and connection from each of them. Take a moment for both sitter and healer to write a few notes, then switch roles. When you've both had a chance as sitter and healer, you can talk about your experiences.

Ask the natural world to collaborate: Ask for permission before picking a flower or a rock or petting a dog or cat. When I first learned this, my teacher Marza would say, "You'll know." But I didn't know. A leaf would catch my eye, and I'd ask, "Will you come with me?" And I'd wait to hear something: a word, a confirmation. After developing a connection with my body, I realized the answers weren't verbal for me but came through bodily sensations. Pets may give you subtle visual cues, such as a tail flick. When they freeze, this is saying no. With nonambulatory nature, such as plants, there are fewer signs to read. I focus on my body's reaction rather than a sound or word.

Try yoga nidra or a body scan meditation, where you move your attention to different body parts. You can also develop your own pattern of moving your attention through the body. When I place my attention on the corpus callosum (the part of the brain in the middle of the head that connects the two hemispheres), the eyes, the heart, the hands, the pelvic bowl, and the feet, I tend to feel the strongest responses.

Engage with your emotions: Give yourself three seconds to be with a feeling when it arises. Notice how you perceive that emotion physically and from where it emanates from in your body. Allow yourself to feel it, even for this tiny, short period. See if you can give it a shape and a name. If you want to try a more in-depth experience to engage with your emotions, learn the Feed Your Demons practice from Tara Mandala, an online international Buddhist community.

Expanding the Network

Practicing mediumship often means exchanging many messages with fellow students. We spend a lot of time thinking of the dead people we know. As we hear *evidence* a medium gives us, our minds sift through possibilities. Mediums typically connect to our "known" dead, or people we knew when they were alive. A subset of the known dead includes the beloved dead, or those select few held especially close to the heart.

Then we have our "named" dead, or those we know by name but didn't ever meet. They can be contemporaries, like Kurt Cobain, or people who came before us, like a great-great-grandma Mary Philips.

These are distinguished from the unknown dead, who are more anonymous people before us—such as those who lived in the house we're in or on the land we're on. We can make up our own rules here. What is helpful in the context of mediumship is to have buckets; for example, someone who can be easily identified (named dead), someone we have a personal connection to (known dead), and those who could represent a group (unknown dead).

Our heritage provides an abundance of dead people to communicate with—the scope of biological inheritance is difficult to fathom. Sifting through genealogy records added depth to some of my ancestry work by showing me where different lines came from and how they intersected. Genealogy research isn't the most accessible activity—it is expensive, time consuming, and puzzle-like, and data quality is often proportional to a person's social standing, so the complete picture is not accurately memorialized. It can provide a lot of data for those who show up in written records, which can fuel your imagination as you work to connect with ancestors.

Learning my ancestry gave me a place in the world. In some ways, I needed to reclaim the past by learning more than the stories I'd been told. If your history is lost to you through any number of displacement traumas (particularly common in the United States are adoption, enslavement, and forced relocation), you may have to work harder and more creatively, with less verifiable data, than others. Explore what appeals to you, what you can access, and what makes you feel alive.

Connect with your living lineage: Do you have loved ones with whom you can talk about death? If so, plan how to contact each other when you're gone. This could be through signs in nature, coincidences, specific memories popping into the mind, or anything that feels meaningful to you both.

Make conversation: Acknowledge verbally or in writing those you consider your ancestors. Celebrate them—maybe even a few of them together. Ask them about their lineages so that your lines extend from your connection to include connections to the past.

Make it simple: Family can be complicated. Step out of it momentarily and ask yourself, whom do you look up to? Who are your heroes, now and in years past? Who are your culture, country, or community's heroes?

Lineage

From the wide breadth of ancestry, we can home into specific lineages that help us trace inheritances or traditions, thereby discovering new people to connect to. A family tree customarily goes back generations. But the lineages we discuss here involve more than the simple lines of the two who came before us, followed by the two before each of them. We all have an infinite and constantly changing number of predecessors. And each will have their network—finding what and who influenced those who influenced us is immediately expansive. We may come across places where lineages connect, or a common progenitor, sometimes in a place we could have never imagined.

Where We Come From

Here are some ways to explore your influences more deeply. While you are imagining your lineages, draw the lines. Be precise—or not. Close your eyes as you imagine, drawing lines around a central character of you. Where do they cross? Where do you have common ancestors across time or space?

Our heart lineages include all those who have touched our hearts—for better or worse. Who have you loved? Who has loved you? Who showed you the ideals of love? What have you spent your life loving?

Our minds' lineage begins with family and the media, ideas, and experiences we were exposed to as children. Then where did you take it? How do you learn with your mind? What have you read, watched, taken in? Where have you studied and with whom? What has caused your mind to soar, and what has helped it know which ideas not to follow? Think through your formal education, then past what you've learned for your jobs, and into the deep stories of your culture and family. Consider fairy tales and myths and legends and theories. What books, movies, shows, and other produced materials have been informative to you? What conversations, interactions, writings, and other spontaneous materials have changed your mind?

The soul or spiritual lineage may take more digging than the others. Start with what feels like "soul" to you. What showed you this feeling? Consider places, people, rituals. When you look at your current set of beliefs, what groups influenced them? What people in which places during what time? How much of your life is from a single epoch in history? How much have you picked and chosen? One of the great gifts of this era is the option of choice. How do you use it?

Who and where makes up your physical lineage? It is not dictated solely by the humans who gave you your genes. Anyone who helped raise you, fed you, or made sure you went outside, had fun, or got rest changed your physical body and could be considered for your lineage.

What stories from your lineages could you commit to physical form? You may want to interview people in your lines or draw them. Perhaps they're already gone, but you could write their stories.

No matter how you look at your lineages, you will find aspects you like and those you wish were not there. Your artistic hero was a misogynist; your eighth great-grandfather was a Loyalist and moved to Canada in the Revolutionary War. We all have dark histories—some closer to the present and some further away. That distance matters, as recent wounds have yet to heal. Tread gently with yourself and the recent past, and reach back until you find something strong and grounding. Ask yourself what came of these lineages. How do they show up in you?

Looking back on the past can bring up a need for grieving, processing, and confronting truths. Grief is intertwined with this work. What does grief feel like for you? How do you engage with it? What resources do you have to support yourself when you're grieving?

There are many processes for conducting formal apologies. If you or an ancestor has done harm, there can be great and small liberation from apologizing. It isn't as simple as saying sorry; these tools can help you navigate the healing process. Look into restorative justice, ho'oponopono, or a twelve-step program to help you make right the past. As you begin to engage in the work of shining light on your dark histories, give yourself time and space to take it slowly.

Versions of Yourself

Every moment we live, we change. Inside ourselves rests our inner dead, who are as previously present and as wholly absent from the corporeal world as any other dead person. They are lovely mediumship contacts because they are familiar, healing, and ever-renewing. There is the common concept of a higher self you can work with, too, and the future versions of you that have yet to come into being.

Carl Jung's concept of the shadow self also offers contacts for mediumship work. These traits, impulses, or needs are considered undesirable, immoral, or socially unacceptable to the conscious self. The active imagination tools of Jungian analysis are like a guided contact experience, providing an excellent precursor to mediumship.

Other-than-Human People

We are used to relating through language. Mediumship with the dead builds on that, but embodied mediumship uses our body's capacity for nonverbal or transverbal data, which is how we can communicate with beings who don't use human language. This includes insects, plants, minerals, and many other beings from Earth. Their communication can be even more subtle but no less meaningful.

The first place that many have already started is with pets. We care for them, interact with them, and notice their wants and needs. We can better relate with them by slowing down and paying attention to the subtle cues they offer in place of words: the position of their ears and tails, where they are looking, and how they move. Our connection with domesticated animals allows for closer physical contact, as animals in the wild typically won't give us a chance to get to know them. If such an opportunity arises, mediumship offers a way to gently, passively open a connection. I learned a lot about communicating with animals and the relationship between people and domestication from Ren Hurst's work, including her book *Wisdom of Wildness* (Findhorn Press, 2023).

Help on the Other Side

Spiritualism has a rich history, built from the rich histories of other traditions, of working with *spirit guides*. We build relationships with these beings in the spirit or other transphysical realms to support our spiritual work. They can be specific people who have passed away or beings who were never human. The two consistent characteristics across all the options are that they are supportive and have more experience than we do. Many Spiritualist mediums work with spirit teams or a spirit band, with different guides performing different functions. The most common role is a control or gatekeeper who decides which spirits can speak with the medium. A scout can help find certain spirits. A doctor or medic can keep watch over the medium's body while they're working. These guides can come to us, or we can seek them out. Like any other relationship, we benefit from clearly articulating our needs and expectations with a spirit guide or guides.

Places

Relating with new places has shown me that how I live my life is only one option—one particular, mostly unquestioned way of being. This revelation helped me be open to mediumship. Once I saw the possibility that so many things I take as normal are strange for someone else, most of the world seemed to be made up of habits people chose a long time ago, many of which are ripe for reconsideration.

On a less abstract level, contact with other traditions also opens new potential. On a trip through India over a decade ago, I stood in a long line of people snaking through a several-stories-tall Hindu temple made of dark stone. There were candles, incense, and colored pastes in every crevice of the structure. All my senses were inundated with ritual. I touched the stones worn smooth by thousands of people who had walked where I walked. Pungent smoke and herbs and flowers filled the air. I didn't have the words for it then, but relating to this religion that was not mine, in a place where I was merely a passer-through, in a moment I understood nothing cognitively, my consciousness was altered.

And we are in a place at every moment of our lives. Each of them is unique and offers a chance for us to build a relationship with it. This is especially true for outdoor places, as they offer the potential to meet with other life forms, beings, weather, and all that makes up the earth. Spending time outdoors is a chance to connect and to feel how they affect our lives.

I have lived in many cold places. One of these is Truckee, California, which I remember reading as a kid had been named the coldest place in the continental United States. My current home is in the so-called "Snow Belt" of western New York. Last winter, nearly forty years into my relationship with cold, I realized it could shift.

I had become hypersensitive to cold, and I found myself highly tense when I was out in it (which is for hours every day with first Nika, then Nika and Coyo, and now Coyo). If a cold wind picked up and whipped through my coat, I would stiffen and feel like I was bracing against an enemy. The realization came when I questioned that impulse. Yes, cold can kill you. But I wasn't in a life-threatening situation. So, instead of bristling at a sudden burst of cold air, trying to shrink my body away, I felt it, letting it hit me. I noticed what the cold did to my body and found it was refreshing, like drinking water.

This new relationship with cold hasn't changed the fact that I prefer to wear gloves, a scarf, boots, and the whole winter getup to take Coyo out in a snowstorm. But I can now be around something that is a constant companion for seven months of the year without feeling like I am in a battle. My interaction with the cold was mediumship. I opened myself to a new way of perceiving a reality where I spent most of my life. The greater natural world deserves such a reassessment from us. This is beautifully articulated in *A Wild and Sacred Call* by Will W. Adams (SUNY Press, 2023), which offers a deep analysis of the importance of our connection to the earth and all its inhabitants.

Look down: You are on some land right now. What is the history of this land? Who has lived here? How did they spend their lives? What are you doing that they may have also done? What are their descendants (if not you) doing now? If you are from a line of colonizers on land that was taken forcibly, how does that impact your relationship with the place and its people? What can you do to acknowledge and heal those past hurts? How can you ensure it does not happen again?

Visit: Pick a place, or a few places, from your lineages to visit either virtually or physically. Spend time in the natural and cultural aspects of the place. Feel the dirt. Eat the food. Talk to the people. Imagine folks from your lineage doing the same. Find where in your current existence the threads of this place began. Barbara Kingsolver said in an interview about *Demon Copperhead*, a modern retelling of *David Copperfield*, that she finally found the way to write the story she'd wanted to tell for years while visiting Charles Dickens's desk: "I had a visit from Dickens, this sort of ethereal visit in his house in Broadstairs, and he told me to tell this story."

Relate with some wild beings: Let your feet relate with grass or mud or sand. Remind your face what it is to relate to the sun and wind and rain. Watch an insect or animal carry out its duties. Even if you are in the city, there is still other-than-human life and wild space (the sky!).

Things

The move to Lily Dale provided a community that changed my life and gave me my first home. I think of my house a lot. I have many feelings about it. Sometimes I'm sitting inside it, surrounded by plain, wide trim made of cherry and ash. Sometimes I'm far away, remembering the feeling of being enclosed in my private space, with thick, black satin curtains drawn to keep the heat in or out. Sometimes, while I'm walking up the street toward the glossy black front door, I'm gazing at its steeply pitched roof, warm gray clapboard siding, tall, double-hung windows with thick white sills, and, depending on the time of year, lots of brown sticks or green leaves all around.

The depth of my relationship with my house has been built by writing its address hundreds of times. My dad's mother's mother first owned the house in the 1910s and passed it down to her daughter. Her daughter did the same with her own. I've emptied it, cleaned every nook and cranny, painted every nook and cranny, repaired its roof, replaced the walls, removed walls, and built new parts. I took down two dying trees from the yard that my ancestors played under as children. It took five years, but they now make up the trim and countertops throughout the house.

I know this building better than any I've ever met and have spent more time here than anywhere else. It isn't a lot for some, but I have moved more than fifty times, and being here for over six years is a record. I've built a relationship with this house through prolonged physical interaction. I've also allowed it to be its own thing. It isn't alive as we define the word, but it has had a life if you consider that it was made and it exists and ages and changes, and will someday cease to exist. When making decisions for it, like choosing the colors of the walls or plants in the yard, I think of what I would like and what makes sense for the house. What fits with it? What does it want? We may not talk in words, but we care for each other. When I walk through my front door, I *feel* something. When I sit inside and take a moment, I notice it hold me.

Marie Kondo's book *The Life Changing Magic of Tidying Up* (Ten Speed Press, 2014) was a sensation. I didn't try it until the depths of the 2020 pandemic, and the book enthralled me. Kondo shows us how to build relationships with the things in our space. She guides us to check with each item we own to see if there's a spark, to respect the items we keep by giving them a proper space to live, and to surround ourselves with the things we love.

AN OBJECT OF YOUR AFFECTION

Think of something you love. If it doesn't exist in the material world, envision it with a corporeal form to help you better relate to each other. For years before this book existed, I imagined it in my hands. As I started writing, I made a tiny clay version of it. I put it on my altar and spend time with it every day.

Notice what kind of data flow in as you touch an item, including what thoughts come up. Try old and new things, and things you made or that strangers made. Try repeatedly switching between items and returning to an item after time to notice shifts.

Pick a series of meaningful objects (such as tarot or oracle cards, things you find in nature, or photographs). Each day, spend a short period quieting, select a single item from the collection, ask the item if you can connect with it, and pose a question. Notice how the response changes with different items and over time.

Interfaces

I spent a year as an altar keeper with Marza's circle. She taught me that altars are interfaces between the physical and other realms. Her use of this specific term was important to me, as I work so much with computer interfaces, the connection between digital and physical worlds. Altars have a rich, ancient history throughout the human experience as ways for us to bring the distant or invisible into reach.

We can think of any material item or place that becomes part of the process as an element of our interface with the beyond. To make an altar, I start with clarity on what I am creating a connection to and why, then invite that being or space to join me through the object and location I've suggested. Sometimes the item or location needs to change. Sometimes items must be added, by noticing what is needed to balance or strengthen the space and asking what is required to support the connection. After the connection has been made, the point of an altar is to tend to it. Altars are not so much works of art to gaze upon, but gardens to keep alive.

BUILD AN ALTAR

Creating ancestor altars is an ancient practice still popular today. Pick a single ancestor or let it be for them all. Consider altars for projects, organizations, causes, places, or time frames. Gather things they like, things that remind you of them, or things they gave you to make an inviting space for you both. Ask those you've chosen to join you at the altar and periodically offer small gifts they may enjoy, such as beloved food items, flowers, candles, or incense. These types of fleeting gifts must be attended to and removed when they are spent. Sit with your altar regularly and allow it to be a place where you connect with your ancestors or other important aspects of your transphysical life.

Healing through Connection

1. Whom do you know who is dead? Are there people from the past you can assume have died, given their ages when you know them? Who is the first person you remember dying when you were young? Which ancestors can you identify by name or description? Whose death stories do you know? Who do you want to speak to, and what do you want to say?

2. Where do you already relate beyond living humans? Did you have an imaginary friend as a kid or any other invisible, private, meaningful relationships that exist only in your mind? This could be anything from a celebrity followed intently but never met to a future dreamed of over and over for decades.

3. What other living beings—from pets to the wild natural world, inanimate objects, figments of your imagination, or beings you cannot meet in person—do you want to get to know?

4. What does your support network look like now if you include people, places, and things? Who supports you? Who helps you expand? Who helps you let go? Are there any gaps? How might you develop connections in these areas?

5. Where do you want to visit someday? What do you hope to encounter there? What places hold special meaning for you? Where do you already have a relationship with place?

6. What is your relationship with the natural world? How do you interact with the outdoors and its inhabitants? What elements of nature are especially important to you?

CHAPTER 6

IMAGINATION AS EXPLORATION

When I say my cottage in Lily Dale was in rough shape when I moved in, I mean *really* rough. It was meant to be a one-season summer cottage, and although my uncle Gary had done some weatherization while he lived in it year-round from 1978 to 1998, that was twenty years before I moved in. When Hannah and I arrived, we cleaned a mountain of ancestral trash out of the living room and scrubbed the floor. We placed the bed alongside the woodstove and set up the projector above it to watch *No One Dies in Lily Dale* that first night. There was no water, and even after we got it turned on, the toilet, the water heater, and the kitchen sink were all broken. We'd use the bathroom at the fire hall across the street and drive forty minutes to a truck stop to take showers. Every morning we'd watch how-to videos, go to Home Depot, try to install whatever we were working on, realize we forgot something, go back to Home Depot, try again, and, sometimes, repeat the entire cycle on a single day. On separate occasions, the water heater and the kitchen sink both flooded the kitchen as I "repaired" them.

The day we arrived in Lily Dale, the temperature barely hit a high of sixteen degrees. In the next month, it rose above freezing for only five days. Until my uncle Gary helped me put in a small 1940s-era, very-out-of-code gas fireplace in the kitchen where all the plumbing was, I had to wake up every two hours to put wood in the fire during the night so the pipes (and I) wouldn't freeze. I couldn't

Imagination as Exploration

leave the house for much longer than that during the day unless the temperature was in the forties, lest the fire go out.

I found it all reasonably charming on my good days—and a battle to win on the bad. I dreamed of what it would be like when I had hot water, central heating, a kitchen counter that wasn't made of warped plywood, floors and windows that you couldn't feel the wind blowing through, electricity in all the rooms, and on and on. I imagined dozens of versions of the kitchen, the exterior, the yard, my bedroom. But as I imagined the changes to my house before I made them, I also started devoting mental energy to what I would do when I had space and time and money after I finished my renovations. I saw myself writing books, throwing parties, and hosting visitors in this simple, cozy, modern—yet filled with character—little cottage.

One of the most common questions new mediums ask is, "Am I making this up?" The most common answer is yes. This is twofold. First, in the same way I dreamed of the renovations for my cottage and the life I would enjoy after they were done, we must *imagine* that we could converse with a dead person. We don't need to believe in it, but we need to feel that it's possible in some realm, even if it is a fairy tale or movie. To this end, try watching mediums demonstrate how it could work. Eventually, you can develop your way of talking to the dead, which could be nothing like what you see in a Spiritualist church or on TV.

Second, imagination is a primary avenue to our internal experience and a safe way to transordinary reality. Mediumship starts inside us. You'll work with all the same materials and processes you always do. You'll eventually expand your mind's available modalities, but what you have right now is what you will work with to start. This is one of the reasons that having the house to work on while I first explored mediumship was a vital counterbalance: it allowed me to move from my internal world into the physical.

Imagination is often thought of purely as a visual process, but there are many modalities to imagining. You can consider using the mind's eye if that feels right, or imagine using sensations or feelings, bodily movement, writing or words, drawing or another way of moving ideas into physical form like sculpting, talking with others, creating stories, conceptualizing relationships or processes, coming up with analogies or metaphors, or a combination of all of these.

I know a medium who is terrific at bringing in the names of his contacts. This is hard for me; I don't think I've ever brought in someone's name during a reading. This medium said that when he was a kid, he read baby name books. He remembers the names of everyone he meets. He's a name person. So it makes sense that he can get names when he connects to spirit. The faculty is already in his head.

In my experience, if I'm wondering if I made it up, I probably did. A more to-the-point question is, what part of my data-processing mind made it up? Was it a bias or projection? Was it my nervous system responding to the environment or the sitter? Did I build an idea out of what I see in the sitter and assume what their life is like? Keep asking and at some point, someday, something will feel different, and you will know you did NOT make that up.

In a circle recently, I felt the chilly weight of being deep underwater and my attention being pulled to smooth, heavy river stones. I thought to myself that it is improbable that one of these four people knows someone who has drowned; this is too dramatic. I pushed my rational thoughts aside and felt into it a bit more. I got the feeling of a woman with a loudness or firmness of character, and she pulled me directly toward one member of the circle with a message about her work. Since circles are for practicing, I decided to share what I saw. It turned out that right before circle, that person had watched a documentary on Virginia Woolf, who drowned herself in a river with rocks in her pocket to weigh her down. Whether Virginia Woolf herself joined in a circle, I psychically picked up on the circle member's recent memories, or it was all a coincidence, what the contact had to say was helpful for the recipient.

Possibly more destabilizing and potentially problematic than making something up is quickly receiving a lot of data you don't think you made up.

Imagination as Exploration

Ontological shock is the disorientation and cognitive dissonance that can occur if our fundamental understanding of reality or worldview is disrupted or challenged. This can happen when we encounter new experiences or information that contradicts deeply held beliefs or assumptions, which can easily occur with mediumship. My example happened recently—after I had established an understanding to support it. I was still alarmed at the clarity of what I received, and I'm not sure how I would have reacted if such precise and confirmed data had come through in my early days. Our minds can only handle so much disruptive content that defies our reality. This is our individual limiting factor.

But what if a meaningful exchange of information with a contact happens and you later cannot verify the information? As in, it felt like you didn't make it up, but perhaps you did. Sometimes sitters forget—I saw a newer medium give a public message to an experienced medium who couldn't identify the contact until four other audience members turned to her simultaneously to remind her who it was. I have heard many stories of mediums having sitters deny information only for them to get in touch hours or days later to tell them they remembered the person or situation the medium had brought through. At other times, we must accept that we are wrong.

Talking to an acquaintance at Sacred Grounds (the coffee shop in Lily Dale) about my house, she suddenly said my uncle was there with us, a tall guy who wanted to send his love from the other side. She asked if she could bring him through for me. I told her that's fine, but my uncle is alive. While it is possible to connect to living people, this wasn't what she meant to do. The only thing that matters when it happens, and it does for everyone, is that we are honest with ourselves and anyone we're working with. The acquaintance said she must have been mistaken, and we continued our conversation. Mediumship can take a quick and scary turn to delusion without humility and trust in our sitters. Holding mediumship lightly and not taking what happens as absolute truth helps, too.

1. Does it matter if you're making it up? What would it mean if you made all of it up or if you had made none of it up?
2. When do you use your imagination? How do you use this skill, and what does your typical imagination effort look and feel like? How long does it last?
3. How do you interact with your internal experience? Not everyone has an internal monologue or a mind's eye and no two internal worlds are the same.

Attention

Every mediumship teacher will tell you to meditate to access your psychic capacities. Mindfulness gives us the gift of presence, which we need to focus our attention. My survey respondents spoke of presence as both a preparatory state and an ongoing condition that facilitates psychic work. It creates the optimal internal conditions for us to access our abilities and connect with energies or information beyond typical perception. Piecing together the many different experiences across practitioners, we find a few themes:

Foundational state: Achieving a state of presence is the first step in most practices. It's a prerequisite for accessing intuitive or psychic abilities.

Heightened awareness: Presence increases awareness of one's body, surroundings, and subtle energies. It allows for attunement to our senses and the present moment.

Mental clarity: Achieving presence often involves quieting the mind and letting go of daily worries and distractions. This mind "space" is essential for receiving communication.

Energetic shift: Many of us feel presence as an energetic and physiological state, accompanied by bodily sensations like tingling, pressure, or a sense of expansion.

Grounding: Presence is often linked to feeling grounded or connected to our surroundings and Earth, which is essential for maintaining balance during work.

Altered perception: Presence changes how we perceive time, space, or our bodies. This is described as feeling "locked in," experiencing a "flow state," or sensing a transphysical expansion.

Emotional regulation: Presence is associated with a sense of calm, peace, or emotional neutrality, which helps maintain objectivity during readings and healings.

Receptivity: Being present can be described as creating an open, receptive state that allows for a better connection with spirit, intuitive insights, or clients' energies.

Focus and concentration: Presence helps us maintain focus and concentration during our work, allowing us to tune out distractions and tune into subtle information.

Embodiment: For many, presence is deeply connected to a sense of embodiment or being fully "in" the body, which allows for further aspects of awareness and reception.

Tethering

I have learned most of my mindfulness skills from the Buddhist tradition, which has a massive and diverse body of practices embedded in philosophies developed over millennia. Mindfulness is not typically considered a skill as much as an unlearning.

The basic structure of a practice of presence is tethering, or attaching, our attention to something (usually the breath) and not getting lost in the natural untethering and retethering that happens. The wandering mind is alluring. If something is uncomfortable, our mind takes us away from it. Our mind takes us back to comfort and familiarity again and again. These are impulses to consider if we take subtle, external input and consciously process it for another person.

Sitting cross-legged with eyes closed is an extreme contrast with our lives. But you can practice presence while making zero changes to your observable behavior. You can tether to an activity when you're doing it. For example, practicing presence with weightlifting has been very helpful for me. My muscles burn, my heart pounds, but I know why, and I have caused these changes in my body on purpose. I show myself I can stay present during challenges when I stay with them.

My mind tends to take me back to anxious thoughts. Noticing my rumination habits and becoming aware of what I come back to again and again in my daily life helps me recognize when it happens during mediumship. Then I can discern if my mind is impulsively moving or receiving data.

GIVE YOUR MIND A VOICE

Carry a notebook for an hour and write down what is happening in your head. Each time you notice a new topic or activity come up, write down how you experience it. Think of all the things that happen inside yourself for a moment. Do you see pictures, hear sounds, or experience feelings and sensations? As you get to know your mind's workings, are there specific topics or activities you would like to experience more?

Explore Your Presence Within

Find some activities already part of your everyday life that you can try tethering to while you're doing them. Brushing your teeth—especially if you have a timer, so you don't have to pay attention to when to stop—is a consistently available option. The next time you brush your teeth, be focused on your tooth brushing. Don't think about it; simply be present with it. If you start thinking, "Is it over yet?" remember you have a timer that will tell you and go back to being only a tooth brusher. Nothing exciting. Nothing revelatory. Just two minutes of presence and oral hygiene.

As I've gotten older, I've developed insomnia. Guided meditations and breathwork help me transition from day to night. Although bedtime can be a natural meditation place, it produces regulation challenges for some people. So if it helps, great, but as always, if not, that's fine too. I lie down and get comfortable, then see how long I can stay present with the breath, counting, or my heartbeat, letting it taper into sleep. When I find I've wandered off, I say, "Oh, I'm thinking again." Then I return my attention to my breath or chosen tether.

Try this also when waking up, before fully coming to consciousness or opening your eyes. When I first notice awareness in the morning, I wiggle my toes, keep my eyes closed, and stay tethered to my breath for as long as I can before the rest of the day seeps in.

Find a practical quantity of time regularly to practice. Consider somewhere between the reasonable extremes of two minutes on the weekend and twenty minutes daily. You'll need to be alone or with another person who is also meditating so that the space is quiet from energetic, visual, and auditory distractions.

Find a physical space for your practice. See what it is like to spend time there, seated, quiet, with nothing to do but be. Try it a few times, making changes as you develop new ideas to make it feel safer and more conducive to presence.

If you come to practice and immediately fall asleep, you may need to catch up on a sleep deficit before you begin a meditation practice. Sleep is a more foundational need than meditation. Rather than practicing presence while fighting off fatigue, use the time you have set aside for meditation to nap, and practice presence during your other daily activities.

The same thing is true for whatever else comes up for you: hunger, sadness, anger, anxiety, fear. Because we are suddenly paying attention to ourselves, something will inevitably arise and that something will feel important. It *is* important. Take note of what it is and allow it to become your focus. Give your body what it asks for. Make sure you're managing your nutrition. Get help with emotions.

Find a balance between using your meditation time to do the same thing each session and exploring new methods. There are meditation apps with guided experiences of any length. Or you can pick a particular song. Try a mantra, chant, humming, poem, or liturgy in your head or out loud. You can count prayer beads or your breath. Try a body scan or journey into the earth or out to space.

When comfortable with your practice, try moving toward an empty version. Try once a week for the same amount of time, and instead of doing anything, you sit and focus on your heartbeat. You can go straight to focusing on the breath if that works for you, but I find I have too much control over the breath, and when I focus on it, I start changing it and thinking about how I breathe, and then my breathing becomes disrupted, which in turn changes my state. So I begin by focusing on my heartbeat, which I cannot control. I often cannot feel my heartbeat unless I have my hand on my pulse or heart at first, then after I catch the beat, I can feel it in my body, and I focus on that.

Time and Place

To better understand our imaginations, we'll need to explore them. One skill to learn is to feel the difference between visiting the past or the future, a place we've been to, or a place that doesn't have an analog.

When we speak of time and place, we invite expansion in a LOT of directions. We can physically move around in our environment and go to other places at the current time. We have the mental ability to remember the past and imagine the future. We have the energetic ability to move our focus from the current place to another place in the current time, including changing scope (moving into a smaller place than the entire body or expanding outside the bounds of the skin).

In theory, we can combine these things to go into different places at different times, but it is difficult to move on two planes. You may find it easier than I do, so pay attention to which dimension you're moving on!

Staying with my friend Joanna Ebenstein for a DIY writing retreat, I was awake for the first few nights thanks to a dog living two doors down who seemed to lament its very existence, often and loudly. I talked with Joanna about it and everything she had tried to remedy the situation. What do you do when the logical avenues have been exhausted, leaving you unable to change something, and you want to?

Late one night, I closed my eyes and sent my attention out of my body, out of bed, through the door, the cement wall, and the neighbor's yard. I peeked my head around, looking for the barking dog.

"Hey, buddy. Can I join you?" He looked at me. I felt a yes.

I walked through the wall and crouched in the yard, not near the dog, but within full view. It was dark. I looked at the dog. He looked at me. He wasn't barking. I felt sad for him. He barked again. I looked away, taking the pressure of my expectations with my gaze. I wondered if there was a stick or ball I could throw for him, but I didn't move to look around. I simply squatted there, focusing on being with my dog friend.

I had practice with this. When I travel and leave Coyo at home, I visit him, doing the same thing. I sit near him, so he knows I love him. I hope it makes him happy and at ease having me near, and it does that for me. That's the thing with this work—I don't know if my dog or the neighbor's dog perceive me or my energy. But it certainly helps me in the situation to handle my emotions, gives me an active outlet for the struggle, and lets me practice my concentration.

It might be imagination, interdimensional travel, or energetic connectedness. I don't know, but emotion, sensations, and visual images fuel my mind. I use great focus and a lot of presence to maintain the connection with wherever I'm visiting. In each case, I treat this attentional travel as real—I don't do anything I wouldn't do in waking life and don't try to change anyone other than myself.

Attentional Travel

Moving through space in the current time is attentional travel. Learning to move your attention around is an essential aspect of focus, and mediumship is simply a specific type of focus. When I'm in a place I want to get to know, the first thing I do when I feel safe enough to close my eyes is to take it in without seeing. A moment of visual quiet to notice what I feel—first in my body, then in the space around me. Then I drop my attention into the ground beneath the place to get a feel for the earth there. Sometimes it is easy to drop in, and my attention tumbles down. Sometimes I can't get a good read; it is too busy. Sometimes it's cooler, warmer, empty, or densely packed with stone. How can I know a place if I haven't closed my eyes there?

Transport yourself: Pick another time or place that inspires you. Find something for each sense other than your eyes—those will be closed. Play sounds or music, potentially loud enough to drown out your location's sounds. Use incense or a diffuser to change the smell of your space. Prepare food with a strong flavor, like peeling an orange or a piece of dark chocolate. Put on silky clothes, draw a hot bath, or step out into the snow. Spend time in this place you've created, eyes closed, allowing your other senses to dominate. Notice what sensations occur in your body. Notice emotions that arise. Notice anxiety or apathy that draws your attention away from the transportation you attempt and ask if it can wait until you've returned. Allow your body to connect with the information your nonvisual senses bring in. Enjoy it until regular life calls you back.

In another's shoes: If there is someone you wish to speak with but they aren't physically present, you can write a conversation out as a dialogue, where you ask questions and they answer. Or improvise it verbally, where you play both roles. Let the conversation proceed in your mind, visualizing yourself talking to them. Often, I like to imagine I am that person. Thinking of what their lives, the highs and lows, might have been like. This can be powerful with problematic or traumatized ancestors if you have the emotional space to engage with them. Putting yourself in their shoes, what would you have to believe to do what they did? How might you have coped with the life they led?

THE ENERGIES AROUND US

Here's a meditation to explore moving our attention into different places and times and allowing it to affect our energy. Remember, you can listen to a recording of this meditation on the Normalize Talking to the Dead website.

First we will take our attention and allow it to drop down through our legs and the floor, sending it into the earth, however far it has to go to get into the actual dirt, into the depths of the planet, where it's solid and ancient. On your next inhale, through that path your attention just traveled, bring strength and energy from within the earth into your body, feeling that security and depth, letting it fill you.

Allow your attention to move back up through the earth and into your feet and legs, up your spine, through your head, and out the top of your crown, into the heavens, into the sky, into the stars. On your next inhale, allow that energy of expansiveness and perspective to fill your body and feel that vastness inside you.

Bring your attention back down to your body. On your next breath, send your attention out in front of you, into the world of living beings. Allow the energy of every living thing within a hundred-foot or -mile radius around you to light up and fill the air with its pulse. Feel that connection to all the life around you, and when you breathe in, allowing the vitality and love of the living world to enter your body, filling your heart.

And as that settles in and swirls around with the strength of the earth and the vastness of the sky, prepare an exhale to take you out through the back of your heart and into the mystery behind you. Allow your attention to wander to the unknown's realms and feel its contribution to life's excitement and cyclical nature. On your next inhale, bring that energy of mystery into yourself, feeling it balance with your energies and those you've brought in from around you.

See if you can find a quiet spot inside your physical being. It could be a toe, your heart, or anywhere you think you can rest your attention for a moment without too much distraction, simply being there, not expecting anything, hanging out. And for anything that comes up—in that spot, your mind, your heart, or your physical body—grab it and set it aside, allowing your attention to be empty, like a marble resting on a floor.

Now take a moment to move backward in time, remembering your state immediately before we sat for this meditation. Moving your entire awareness to that position in time. Remember comes from the Latin rememorari, which means "to call to mind." We generally use it to refer to something that has come from the past, but we can also use it to think of and envision the future. Unlike forecasting or foretelling the future, premembering, like remembering, is something of a subjective experience. It isn't about being right, but having a connection to a time and place.

Call to mind the moments after you finish this meditation. Just one or two. Where your body will move to in space. How you might feel once there. Using our imaginations to look into the future can bring us hope, facilitate change, expand our potential, or simply feel comforting, inspiring, and intriguing.

Allow your attention to return to the present moment. When you are ready to engage the thinking mind and external world again, allow your attention to go into your eyes and open them, connecting back to your room.

The Rest of Life

It is true that during that trip to Joanna's, the neighbor's dog quieted down every time I could fully place my attention with him. The rest of the story is that he still barked a lot. I eventually lost interest in spending time with him energetically because that took more effort than ignoring his barking. I needed to keep my eyes open and attention with my body because I wanted to be where I was—chopping onions for dinner or simply hanging out with Joanna. If I tried to put only part of my attention with the dog, it didn't produce any effect.

The day-to-day reality of this work is that it isn't practical most of the time. It is frosting on the cake of life—not the cake itself. It might be the flame on the candle and the confetti in the frosting, too. The bright, shiny feature brings it all together and *makes it a cake.* It's not a practical solution for every issue.

Whenever you go to a place in your imagination or with your attention, return to an ordinary state when you're done. This is one more skill to learn, and remembering it can be a challenge. Although we can have impact in our imaginations, we live in physical reality. If we bypass the physical for the spiritual for too long, we risk our connection to other people, nature, and our lives.

Energetic resolutions: Try imagining someone you miss or a situation you feel lost about. Get safe and comfortable and ask yourself to show up as the most loving version of yourself. Find your way from your current place to a neutral space and mentally ask the person, situation, or being you need to work with if they will join you there energetically. Then be present. Listen. Hold your energy in the situation, allowing it to be whatever it is without changing it. Part of the effectiveness of this technique for me is practicing holding my attention without will, manipulation, wanting, or pushing.

Vantage points: When imagining, try looking directly out of your own eyes, viewing yourself from above or below, or watching from a vantage point. Which is easiest for you? Which is the hardest?

Tiny time travel: How does your body feel when you close your eyes and imagine the present around you? What might be happening that you can't see? What if you imagine the same place, but one minute in the past or future? Try this alone and with others. Feeling slight changes in the timeline helps us develop a feeling for them before we move further into the past or future.

Direct from book to movie: While reading or being read to, slowly build the world and the action in your mind, stopping to fill in details that aren't in the text. This is especially fun with a book not set in the current time or place. Notice how much imagining happens when you read and what it takes to expand on that foundation.

Develop your mind's eye: I learned this exercise twice—once from Andrea Wadsworth and again as *trataka* when I studied yogic meditation. Andrea had me spend several months imagining a tangerine. A couple of times a day, set a timer for at least thirty seconds, then work your way up to a few minutes. Grab something bright and visually simple, like an orange. Put it directly in front of your face to get a good look, then close your eyes and keep seeing it. As soon as you lose the image, open your eyes and look at the physical object again. Enjoy the tricks your mind plays on you; write them down to learn what it has up its sleeve.

Revisit the past: If you find yourself particularly resourced, try visiting a challenging memory. Not the most difficult memory, but a tiny moment when you wish you'd done something differently or that someone else had done something differently. Imagine yourself coming in as you are now and either doing what you'd hoped for or asking the other person to do what you'd hoped for. Notice the difference in your imagination when it is emotionally charged.

Map out your upcoming year: Each day between Christmas (December 25) and Epiphany (January 6), divine for an upcoming month of the new year. I started with pulling tarot cards and writing a few sentences, but I have experimented with songs, dreams, multiple tarot decks, runes, colors—anything meaningful with at least twelve options. Each day, you can use the objects to make a monthly collage for the background of your phone or save your intpretation of them as a voice recording to listen to on the first of each month.

CHAPTER 7

MEDIUMSHIP FOR MONEY

In the early spring of my first year in Lily Dale, I became very ill. Following an afternoon cleaning out the attic, I got a fever for a few days. It made all the effort I expended to warm and feed myself in my very needy cottage nearly unbearable, but it passed, and I forgot about it. Later that year, a couple of weeks into a month and a half in western Kenya, I got malaria, for which I was treated immediately. Still, fevers kept me in bed, this time while managing a ten-person research team tasked with 200 highly sensitive interviews in ten days. When we finished and I returned to California to complete the project, I became feverish and landed in the emergency room within a day. After that, I went to my parents' house in Nevada City to recuperate my strength so I could travel back to New York. After another week, my temperature was up again and I was back in the ER.

When I finally returned to my house in Lily Dale, nearly four months after I left, I couldn't make it through a day without a nap or a week without a fever. I had hundreds of tests done, and nobody had any idea what was wrong with me or how long it would take to get better, instead offering me Tylenol and antidepressants, neither of which I took. I lived alone in a marginally inhabitable home, had no savings, and couldn't work more than a couple hours at a time. I was terrified for my future and the beginnings of financial stability I'd worked so hard to build. I don't remember having conscious thoughts of it, but when I look back, I was filled with fear about my consulting business surviving and most of my neighbors had the same job: medium.

I had done a few tarot readings for money over the years, and after seeing all the readers spring up on social media, I did the math to see if I could live on it. It was immediately apparent that it would be tough without a considerable client base, and I knew mediumship would be no different. Although psychic services make up a two-billion-dollar industry in the United States, and the share of mediumship grew from 18 to 25 percent between 2018 and 2021, it is not an easy business. Attempting to explain the nature of consciousness is challenging, but writing about providing spiritual services within a capitalist framework is even more problematic. There is a similarity in that I don't have definitive answers, and we need to look at the issue collectively and individually.

In addition to my research and experience, I draw on my conversations with three friends who have deeper knowledge of working as a professional medium. Grace Kredell is an artist, psychic practitioner, community organizer, and historian who wrote her graduate thesis on the labor issues facing occult workers, mostly women of color, in nineteenth-century New York City. Dr. Michelle Barr started as a therapist before becoming a transformation coach specializing in the personal challenges mediums and other healers face in making their spiritual work a career. Celeste Elliott has been a registered Lily Dale medium and resident for fourteen years.

Spirituality and money have a sordid relationship, and much of your previous cultural knowledge of mediumship for money has likely been colored by high-profile stories of fraud, coercion, and deception by spiritual and religious leaders and communities. This is underscored by a legal gray area around professional mediumship. Proving the authenticity of magic, supernatural abilities, and occult powers in the courts fell out of favor after the Salem witch trials. It was replaced with a money-centric approach focusing on prosecuting fraudulent providers. The current New York state fortune telling law restricting using "occult powers" was enacted in 1967 as a theft-related offense. This can be compared to the United Kingdom, which, in a 2008 Consumer Protection from Unfair Trading Regulations, placed mediumship within the same regulatory context as all business services.

United States law fails to offer mediumship the respectful position of a business service. This leaves providers feeling dismissed and consumers unprotected. Professional mediums often use either a disclaimer that their work is for entertainment or frame payment as an optional donation. First Amendment protection technically applies to those practicing mediumship as part of their religion, but there is no explicit legal tie, even for Spiritualism.

Because the role is often inhabited by people with marginalized identities, getting fair legal treatment has been an issue for mediums as long as it has been a profession. As we've seen, mediumship has been primarily women's work in the United States during the past few centuries. Providing any care service is not just usually women's work, but poor women's work. And with any history of anything in the United States, you know that race plays a role.

Do we need to talk about gender, race, and class to get through a little chapter on money in a book about mediumship? Yes. Do I have what it takes to get us through this conversation? Probably not. But I will offer what I can.

Lily Dale is a difficult place to make your home. I lived here for five years before it finally dawned on me why there aren't more young residents. In Lily Dale, you must be a card-carrying Spiritualist to own a house, and we don't own the land our houses sit on. We have ninety-nine-year land leases with the Lily Dale Assembly. That might not seem like a big deal, but banks cannot provide mortgages if they cannot seize and resell the house when borrowers don't pay them back. Lacking a Spiritualist bank to give loans, most people here pay for their houses in cash.

This keeps house prices artificially low, especially when combined with a minimum one-year process to become a member of the Assembly. Then there is a minimum two-year process (which I have not yet undertaken) to become a registered medium so that you can do readings in person on the grounds. During those two years before you test, you must remain in the Dale for at least a few weeks to complete dozens of required services. So, who has the money to buy a house in cash in a place where the employment rate is one-third of the rest of the state and wait a few years before they can earn money again? It helps to have a paid-off house to sell and a fixed income to live on. And then there are the lucky few like me who inherit a house.

I saw my older, sometimes quite elderly, neighbors support themselves as part-time mediums, and I saw a job I could manage. Illness, age, and unusual schedules are not unsurmountable problems for a potential medium. In addition to having a much older population than the rest of the state and country, 29 percent of our residents are disabled, as compared with 13 percent in New York State. Mediums can make their own schedule and work by phone (or, these days, video calls) and not go anywhere at all.

If you aren't trying to be a registered Lily Dale medium, which requires an extensive interview, background check, and testing process, being a medium doesn't usually require a degree, certificate, or résumé. It does involve years of investment in training and practice. For most, this is done while working at another job to support oneself, as there is no financial aid or student loans for mediumship school. It also requires caring for strangers through one-on-one, face-to-face experiences. This is taxing work before you even bring the psychic part into it.

I'm not saying everyone who does mediumship is backed into a corner, especially people who have jumped through all the hoops to be a Lily Dale medium. But it is a hard job that people don't always have as their first choice. If someone works as a medium or other type of care worker, they may be in a financially vulnerable position due to the structural inequities of our economic system, which put women and minority genders, people of color, those who are disabled or chronically ill, and many other people at a disadvantage. We have a culture that doesn't pay well for care. So the people who do care work tend not to make much money at it. And who takes jobs that don't pay well? It isn't people who have surplus funds.

Mediumship, tarot, psychic, astrology, and other occult workers have another issue to deal with on top of the standard care work struggles of low pay and a demanding job: it is typically a career where you need to work for yourself. Industry reports always include market share, where the largest companies are mapped out. The IBISWorld report on psychic services says, "There are no companies that hold a large enough market share in the Psychic Services in the US industry to include." This is comparable to other personal services industries, where many businesses are run by a single individual, such as cleaning and repair providers, tutors, trainers, and massage therapists. This isn't necessarily a bad thing, but it requires additional skills to run a business.

This is where Lily Dale becomes a bit of a utopia. It offers normalization of the work, a registration process to give mediums legitimacy, and a physical location to aggregate clients. Almost like a workers' cooperative, the place does the advertising, and the mediums offer public demonstrations to show their capacities. We have a few hundred people a day wandering around for ten weeks a year, looking for a reading. Registered mediums work for themselves, still dealing with self-employment taxes and small business insurance. Lily Dale handles the marketing part. And although it is still not an easy job, there is also the camaraderie of living and working in physical proximity. Many mediums and other types of healers I know outside the Dale are not part of such a highly connected community, making it a lonelier endeavor.

So now that we have a little background on the economics of mediumship, let's talk about getting paid for it. It seems straightforward: we spend our energy caring for a person during a reading; this is work, and we should make money, and probably good money. In Lily Dale, these days, it is around $100 for a half-hour reading by a registered medium. For each session, you need to add a bit of time for logistics and admin and a time buffer for preparation and aftercare. So that half-hour reading takes up at least an hour of the medium's time. In Lily Dale, the mediums are also required to volunteer dozens of hours, typically doing public demonstrations each season, further reducing the time available for private readings.

A typical schedule might be four readings a day, six days a week, for the ten-week season, which would total $24,000. The rest of the year would see significantly less demand. Plus, there are inevitable no-shows, off days, the 3 to 5 percent for credit card processing fees, a few thousand in Lily Dale costs, insurance, a website, taxes, ongoing education, and other business expenses. That might sound okay in the abstract, but I do not have the immense mental, physical, emotional, and spiritual fortitude to do twenty-four readings a week. For me, a realistic load would be at most half that. And that would be in a scenario in which Lily Dale supported me in finding clients, a luxury most mediums do not have.

Let's return to some of our societal issues that contribute to that need for fortitude. When I say mediums have been stigmatized in the past, accusations have fallen into four main categories. You will recognize them as commonly used insults against those who do not behave as expected:

* Intellectual capacity
* Morality
* Honesty
* Sexualization

There aren't many careers that could potentially get you called a hysterical, fraudulent, possessed slut, but mediumship—at least historically—could. Exposure to bias and societal pressure contributes another layer to this already challenging undertaking.

It is a lot easier not to make it your job. And in case all this wasn't enough, I have more reasons. As anyone who monetizes their creativity or has made their side hustle into their main gig knows, money adds pressure. When you depend on something to make sure you have a home, food, and health care, you no longer have a choice about doing it. This can create a psychological challenge for any type of work, but we're talking about depending on your ability to speak to the dead to pay the bills. A more sustainable option would be to work as a counselor or educator. If you *need* the beyond, it can take a toll. While it is always there, we aren't meant always to be there.

Each of us experiences and reacts to legal ambiguities, financial strain, structural inequities, and professional pressure differently. These issues mingle with our intergenerational and personal issues of self-doubt, self-worth, money, care, and spirituality. Those who pursue professional mediumship work may contend with what Michelle Barr calls "noble suffering." The interplay of these wider conditions with our individual experience can manifest as imposter syndrome, chronic undercharging, and burnout.

Facing all this daily requires a lot from a person. Professional mediums are brave and strong people. Their work provides a unique source of solace and inspiration for many. The world could do with more humans who can dedicate their lives to becoming safe, reliable, accurate, compassionate communicators with the beyond.

---

1. What stories have you seen, read, or heard regarding other people's experiences with spiritual professionals or religious clergy? Do you generally feel positively, negatively, or indifferent about them?

2. What direct experiences have you had with spiritual professionals or religious clergy? How does that affect your feelings about working with them? Serving as one?

3. What cultural changes in ideals, legislation, or customs might improve your desire to work with or become a spiritual or religious provider?

PART III
GIVING RISE TO MEDIUMSHIP

At last, we have arrived at the *how* of mediumship. We have explored a constellation of skills involving and unifying the mind, body, and spirit. We have developed language for parts of life you might have sensed but didn't quite have the words for. Now we make something amorphous into a concrete set of steps to walk. The point is not to do them once and produce a magnum opus or to follow them to the letter and become a perfect master of steps. Instead, we ritualize relationships, embodiment, community, mindfulness, and creativity.

Before we start, here is an overview of what I've used to build a safe and effective practice:

1. **A long tradition:** There are many people, places, and resources from which to learn. Gather the information needed to feel prepared. Many traditions, including American Spiritualism, shamanism, voodoo, and Wicca, delve deeply into the dynamics of relationships with the beyond.
2. **Accountability:** This requires more than good intentions. By acting as mediums, we take responsibility for what we communicate, how we communicate it, and our process from beginning to end.
3. **Interdependence:** The human experience offers us a chance to be singular beings without controlling parts of others or having parts of

ourselves controlled. This opportunity exists in a vehicle (body) made from Earth. We cannot disconnect from its web of support and needs.

4. **Focus on the physical:** We always have a place here. This is where we begin and end the practice, no matter how far beyond we go. Remember to apply these skills in the material realm first.

5. **We live here:** Humans exist in the physical world, and it is our realm. If something feels off, take your feelings seriously. We always have the right to say, "NO." When in doubt, return to the body and physical space and tell everything else to leave.

6. **Boundaries:** It is easier to keep out what you don't want around than to get it to leave after it is present. Using correct energetic, physical, and emotional boundaries—knowing where we end and others begin—is essential with every type of connection.

7. **Starting from full:** The more we accept our wholeness, even the parts we don't like, the less room there is in ourselves (energetically, mentally, on all planes) for others to come in uninvited.

8. **Choose care first:** When we struggle, don't feel well, or have fear or insecurity, we can use our tools of care and discernment to assess and create a plan to make it through. When in doubt, start with a simple check: Have I slept enough? Have I eaten enough? Am I hydrated? Do I need time away from or together with other humans? Can I discern between corporeal and transphysical reality?

9. **Reach out:** You may want to find a friend (or several) and do the exercises in this book together. Check the Resources section and the NT2TD website to find events or groups to join.

10. **Reach in:** Know that resistance will show up. We're seeking flow here, which requires both push and pull. Be curious. Ask yourself if you want to play. Notice what you want, then listen.

CHAPTER 8

FORMING METHODS

My first fall in Lily Dale, still in poor health, I heard of the Fellowships of the Spirit school of prophecy and spiritual healing. I signed up for the required intro course, Spiritual Insight Training, on the day my friend Daniel Rekshan recommended it. Eager for the structure and constant encounter with new information that school offers, I didn't think very deeply about the reality of joining a rigorous two-year program. By the end I felt like I had been back to graduate school. Much of the Fellowships' approach is unique and highly adapted to teaching mediumship and healing in the modern world. One of the things that most captured my attention was how they supported our learning process with dozens of lectures and demonstrations by mediums. Through note-taking rubrics and discussion (as well as, I'm guessing, how they prepped the teachers), they encouraged us to pay attention to three aspects of each medium's work: their beliefs, their order of operations, and how they used their bodies. This meant we were exposed to many different backgrounds and styles, and not superficially. With these deeper conversations and broader observations, we could see behind the words and choose the best aspects for us.

I wrote this book as another way to provide such an approach. When you read these steps, I hope you will know what they mean, feel empowered to try them, and then use them to develop your own. Following is my complete meth-

Forming Methods

odology, a structured and repeatable framework to help produce consistent and reliable results. Throughout the rest of the book, you'll be prompted to develop, test, and evolve your process. Please change, shorten, or elaborate it as you work.

1. Quiet.
2. Connect: confirm that the mind, body, spirit, and environment are appropriate for connecting. Verbally confirm consent with the sitter (if applicable).
   - Move attention to the space around the self.
   - Move attention to the self.
   - Move attention to the sitter (if applicable).
   - Move attention to the contact point.
3. Ask.
   - Confirm consent with the contact and share intention.
   - Engage in dialogue.
4. Receive: notice what is happening in the mind and body while attention is at the contact point.
5. Translate.
   - Express the information.
   - Ask the sitter if they understand what has been said (if applicable).
6. Repeat.
7. Close.
   - Thank then withdraw attention from the contact.
   - Thank then withdraw attention from the sitter (if applicable).
   - Bring all attention back to the self.

You can go through this process one step at a time, read all the steps, then return to the exercises. We open a connection, make space for something to come through, move that thing out of our internal worlds and into the external world, and repeat until we're ready to close the connection.

Quieting

I spent much of the past decade feeling like the world was telling me to let go. I couldn't understand why I kept getting this advice. I have left countless homes, people, jobs, and hobbies. But letting go is more than a physical act; it is a mental and emotional process.

Presence teaches us to release the pull and stay where we are, whether that pull is toward zoning out or emotional release. The information we're dealing with in the transphysical world is subtle. I will miss it if I can't stay focused on almost nothing. In other words, boredom and drama are stronger pulls that are sometimes out of our control based on our neurological state. But I can't get to that subtle other without the ability to drop them. And with the dead, we often deal with intense emotions of grief, love, and loss. If I am liable to be pulled into emotional turmoil and have no way to stop it, I will be unable to provide meaningful messages to or from others; it will all end up being about myself.

If we hope to use connecting through mediumship, we must learn to make some mental space. We cannot hear others speaking if we have constant inner dialogue. This is true in verbal conversations: we must stop talking at least occasionally so the other person can be heard.

External Factors

To practice connection through mediumship, we need a place where we are free from potential harm from the elements and other beings. In a paper on polyvagal theory and spiritual practices, Dr. Stephen Porges writes, "In order for the positive benefits of contemplative practices to be experienced, the rituals associated with contemplative practices (e.g., chants, prayers, meditation, and dance) must be performed in a context defined by physical features that are calming and soothing and promote feelings of safety." This can include sounds, smells, light, or other sensory cues. Suppose we are already in a vulnerable physiological state or not in a safe context free from potential predators and distractions. In that case, meditation, prayer, breathwork, yoga, etc., can trigger a defensive state because our body does not feel safe moving attention away from the potential danger it senses. So give yourself a break if meditation, visualization, or breathwork don't feel right sometimes.

People have built temples for their sacred practices throughout the ages, which may have had more than aesthetic purposes. A foot of stone surrounding the body, with only a single entrance, helps ensure protection from interruption and harm. Those thick walls also serve as a barrier to sound, light, and movement. Mediums often work in darkened rooms and sometimes use actual cabinets, sitting within small, enclosed spaces during séances.

Internal Factors

Ever wonder why you get the best ideas when drifting off to sleep? Or on a walk or in the shower? These are moments of internal safety where the mind has the freedom to let thoughts arise and fall away without goals or restriction. As we cultivate space in ourselves, a stillness where thoughts, feelings, and sensations are allowed to come and go as they please, these subtle messages can arise. This is where letting go becomes so important. If we stop the flow of information by holding on to a specific part of the experience, we bring the thinking mind back into play.

To find an internal quiet is to be in a state of observation. My favorite metaphor for this is a forest floor. The next time you walk outside, look at the ground before you. You might notice leaves and sticks and various ground-y things. Take a moment to kneel and focus your eyes on a small area. It will come alive. There will be dirt and potentially all sorts of tiny creatures moving around. There may be small plants you didn't notice before; the ground is no longer a uniform color or shape but comprises hundreds of differently sized and textured particles. Shifting focus opens up a whole new world to behold.

SETTING YOURSELF UP FOR QUIET

Here's a meditation to support quieting.

Find a stable, comfortable, balanced position. You won't be moving for a few moments, so ensure you have good blood flow to your limbs.

If you fall asleep, don't worry. Find your comfy spot, feet flat on the floor. Close your eyes if you'd like, and start noticing your breath. Find a place for your hands that feels comfortable. I usually put my hands palms down on my thighs. If I'm connecting, I might put the palms up, but right now, we are quieting, and I will put the palms down.

Inhale as long as you can. You can breathe in through your nose or mouth, whatever is comfortable. Start in your belly, then expand your chest. When you're ready, exhale as long as you can. Take a few cleansing breaths like this, allowing your spirit, your complete awareness, to enter your body.

You are recalibrating through the internal world, away from the device or book in front of you. Focus on the sounds around you. Hear what you can in your physical space. The hum of a device, appliance, or fan, creaks of floorboards, a pet or another person in a nearby room, trees blowing in the wind. Notice those faraway sounds. And then, as you move in closer, notice what fills up the sound waves around your body, imagining what they might look like as they hit your ears.

Next, feel the boundaries of your skin. Notice the air temperature, the humidity levels, and your overall temperature. Are you feeling warm or cool? Can you perceive temperature variations between extremities and your core or different body parts? Take a deep breath in with your nose and notice any smells. Is the air strong or soft? Is it more savory or sweet? Is there anything distinguishable in those scents? Or is it a general smell? Check if there's any taste lingering in your mouth, like from a meal or beverage. Is your mouth dry, or are you thirsty?

As you move into the body, bring your focus right behind your eyes, as if you are looking out but without seeing anything; allow that focus to move into your mind, into the center of your brain, seeing what comes up there. Watch thoughts, ideas, plans, memories, to-do items, or anything else come up, and let them float away once you've noticed them. If they don't leave on their own, imagine you can gently pick them up and put them in a little basket, saving them for later, in case they are needed. Stay here, letting the mind flow until nothing else comes up and a quiet emerges.

Allow your focus to expand to your whole physical body. Notice any sensations, fullness or emptiness, dark or light. Allow your attention to go wherever there are sensations, feeling them in their place, then expanding back to the body as a whole. If a particular pain or feeling cannot dissipate with your attention, imagine gently scooping it up and setting it in your basket for later, creating a quiet in the body for the moment.

Allow your attention to narrow into your chest, alongside your heart. Be there. Take a feel around for any emotions—old ones, fresh ones, current ones. Give each one a nod and a wave, letting it fall away. If some persist, let yourself be with them until they subside, or you can scoop them out and put them to your side in your basket, knowing you'll have time to observe those emotions, to spend time with them, to recognize and work through them in another moment.

When you're ready, expand your attention to your entire being, letting your focus soften. Enjoy the quiet until you are prepared to return to the external world.

EMERGING SILENCE

The next time you have a moment of quiet, try closing your eyes and letting go of anything that is not nothing.

Move your attention into unusual but quiet places: outer space, the depths of the earth, inside your body, under the sea, or anywhere else you imagine a quality of silence. Allow yourself to "listen" and imagine what you might hear there.

If you cannot find quietness, look back to your self-soothsaying deck or the tools you've developed to shift your nervous system state. Also consider reading Justin Michael Williams's book *Stay Woke: A Meditation Guide for the Rest of Us* (Sounds True, 2020).

Asking

Now we open the connection and ask a contact to join us. The first contact is always the self. We must firmly connect to ourselves before we connect to energy from outside ourselves. Being truly with ourselves is our best way to maintain discernment; with discernment comes safety and openness. Working on that self-connection may be all that is accessible some days. When you find that presence, you can choose a resting point (I often use my heart) and throughout the process, if things feel unclear or you are unsure of something, return to it to check in.

We ask for a few reasons and in a few ways. The first is to open the connection. We ask permission. May I do this work? May I sit here? Before any outward asking, we ask ourselves: Is this mine to do? Is this when and where I want to do this? We find an inner alignment. This doesn't need words, but instead feeling into: Am I safe right now? For myself and others? If not, what might help move me toward safety?

Once we have prepared ourselves, we check with our environment. In the ceremony and ritual I learned from Marza, we always asked the place before we began. There is no connection without permission, consent, and invitation: with ourselves, our surroundings, and the other.

In the form of *I Ching* divination that I learned, we began each session by asking if we could ask the question we'd brought. If the response was no, we reformed the question or moved on to another. This is an alignment practice. Are my energies of heart, mind, spirit, and body aligned? Am I saying what I'm genuinely asking? Practicing this with a tool such as a pendulum, tarot card, or coin is especially helpful. The answer is external and requires no interpretation: we are asking a yes or no question.

The next type of asking is an invitation. At the outset of connection, clearly articulating what I plan to do and why helps ensure the beings I invite in are safe and helpful. I learned the subtle difference between intention and invitation from Stargazer Li, a wise teacher, time traveler, and guide to the night sky with whom I took classes for several years. In this practice, the whole point is to get out of our own way, so we invite those who can support what we embark upon and leave out those not in alignment with our purpose. An intention is included in the invitation, but as a way of informing contacts so they can decide to join or not, rather than telling them what to do.

The last type of asking is the interview. This happens within the connection. Questions can be technical: please talk slower, louder, in pictures and not words, in words and not pictures. What does this mean? I only see darkness; can you show me more? Is this what you want me to know/see/understand/share? We embark upon communication to engage with the being on the other side. We initiate the connection; we ask for their input. It is our responsibility to hold up our end of the bargain. It is our responsibility to ask for what we need.

Identifying

We do not have to know where our inspiration comes from to feel inspired. We do not have to verify the source of our connection, only that the intention behind the contact is safe. However, it is validating to have proof occasionally, and if we move on to message work or readings, we must learn identification. It supports the development of relationships so we can work safely and know whom to thank and for whom to ask.

The process is strengthened by developing our discernment. We will need other people to help validate the reality we present, but first, we need the confidence to say that reality out loud. To learn the identification of contacts, we need to work with others. To prepare for that, we can begin to identify how different types of data form within ourselves.

Receiving

Ultimately, we hope to receive some message, inspiration, or confirmation. Our goal is information that doesn't come from us figuring it out or deducing it. When we receive information while in connection, it feels different than something we come up with on our own because it appears seemingly out of nowhere, comes in as a sensation unrelated to our environment, or is otherwise unexpected.

Translating

Data in our minds must be externalized for us to share it. If we aim to create something that others can see, hear, or touch, we must find a way to get it out of ourselves. This part of the process is natural to any artist. Expression is a key aspect of art and relating and is a skill. We might want to keep what we have inside, whether from our imagination or given to us by spirit. This step may be straightforward, almost invisible to you, or stunningly complex, stopping the whole process.

Our expressive abilities make a difference, and working with different forms at different skill levels helps illuminate the process and what is holding us back. Explore playing the piano to voice your sorrows when you are not familiar with the instrument and feel what it means not to be able to translate. There is a gap between receiving (whether a message from a spirit or an emotion from your heart) and translating. This is our filter: Is it okay to express this? How do I want to express this?

THE SPECTRUM OF CONNECTION

Explore how different information feels when you receive it. Work with a contact in the physical world—a person, animal, or otherwise tangible being.

Logic: Use your rational mind to deduce a fact about the contact.

Empathic: Tap into your feeling self to experience emotions the contact could be feeling.

Psychic: Quiet and allow data to flow through yourself, putting your hand on the contact and acknowledging what comes in at that moment to be received psychically.

Mediumistic: Move your attention to a contact point and ask a spirit or outside entity to give you a piece of data about the contact.

GETTING ANSWERS

Here's a meditation to feel how your mind and body produce data:

Start to arrive in your body. Notice the space around you and tune in first to the sounds in your room, building, and street. Keep your attention outside your mind and body, out all around you, trying to pick up all the noise you might hear over the next few moments, noting them so that your nervous system knows to ignore them. So pick up on a fan, street noise, or someone walking, noting those noises that may occur, and turn their volume down.

Allow your attention to come inside your body through your breath. Allow your belly and your lungs to fill and feel the tension of your skin shifting. Allow your focus to move through your body and into your arms and legs, then into your hands and feet. Wiggle your toes and fingers, sending your attention into twenty places at once.

And then go into the middle of your brain. And as you sit in that neutral place, I will ask you some questions. And notice where the answer comes up. We've sat in a few different parts of our bodies, in other areas in our minds, but know there are hundreds more places inside and outside ourselves for information to enter. Notice the first thing that happens after I ask the question, whether it's an itch on your forehead, a reminder of what someone forgot to do, or an answer to the question that makes sense or doesn't. Anything counts, whatever it is.

We will only notice the answers, not process them, not write them down, not save them. So clear yourself; with a deep breath, you can pin your attention into the middle of your brain. And then answer this.

What did you have for breakfast? And the answer isn't important, but what came up? Did you have to sift through some things to get to something? Did a feeling of fullness in your belly come? Did a picture of what you ate appear?

What color is the steering wheel of the last car you drove?
How long are your fingernails?
What's five times seven?
Do you like banana custard?
What's your favorite radio station?
What did you look like when you were five?
What's your favorite shirt?
What was the last present you received?
When is your birthday?
How do you sign your name?
What do you want to eat for lunch tomorrow?
When do you need to go grocery shopping next?
How much was your last electricity bill?
What's your favorite song to sing?
How do you put on a shoe?
Who was the thirty-second president of the United States?
What's your favorite kind of ice cream?
When was the last time you high-fived someone?
What was the first day of fourth grade like?
What will you do next year?
Do you own a scarf? What do you look like when you wear it?

Expand your awareness into the rest of the body and mind. Allow yourself to come back to the external world and open your eyes.

Change your filters: Explore how many filters you turn on or off. Explore who gets to experience your expressions: nobody, strangers, friends, lovers. Explore translating from image to image, image to word, feeling to image, and seeing which are comfortable. If you speak multiple languages, try switching between them. Try your most conservative or most permissive self.

WWJD: Pick a person in spirit whom you know enough about that you can imitate their physicality. Stand up and walk around as they might. Talk like they would. Move as you imagine they moved. Write or draw as if you are them.

Time decoration: Pick a few songs in different genres to which you have a strong emotional or bodily reaction. Play them one after another and allow yourself to dance, draw, or write from them. Let the songs be your contact and let them dictate how you move and express yourself.

Closing

There is always the question of when to finish. There is no right or wrong here; the connection can always be reopened. Sometimes I stop a connection when I get an idea and move into creating with the connection closed. In readings for others, I translate within the connection, allowing my filters to turn off and let the information flow out rather than be a conversation in my head. Sometimes, with a very concrete project, I'll open the connection and leave it open for the days I'm working on it, closing after I've finished.

When I've finished the connection or have something else I need to do, I resist the urge to immediately move on. I take a moment to close the connection and thank everyone who participated (myself included) for the experience. Closing the connection is not only for my self-maintenance, to ensure my energy isn't leaking away or others aren't leaking into me; it also strengthens my relationships. Closing can be as elaborate or simple as your opening invitation, the same thing in reverse, or a different form. Just don't forget it! I sometimes do. Then I close when I remember.

A metaphor from the mundane world: I am not tidy. I tend to let the dishes pile up. When I come into the kitchen for the first time in the morning to a sink full of dirty dishes, my energy for the current day gets used for tending to (or ignoring) the dishes from the day before. If I spend a few minutes cleaning up at the end of the day (or better yet, after each meal), I get to stay in the present moment. Mediumship is similar. Keep the connection tidy by closing it whenever not in use. This is a type of *energetic hygiene*, or the maintenance of good boundaries between ourselves and the unseen world.

Habit Formation

People sometimes wonder how I got into mediumship so quickly, and the unsexy answer is that I did it all the time from the moment I was introduced to it. Only some people need, want, or are able to do that. I did it because I was curious, and living in Lily Dale made mediumship a significant part of my social life.

GET THE HANG OF OPENING AND CLOSING

Here are a few ways to get in the habit of turning your connection on and off.

1. Turn your opening and closing of the connection into physical activities—try a few. Light a candle to open and blow it out to close. Make a few specific hand motions and use them reversed to close.

2. Turn a specific chair or spot into a mediumship-only zone, imagining a portal to the spirit realm you access when you sit in it. Visualize yourself opening the connection as you enter the space and closing it as you leave it. You can always turn it back to regular space when you're done experimenting.

3. Practice opening and closing all sorts of activities—meals, workouts, hangouts, relaxation, etc.

Healthy habits form through diversity of activities, repetition over time, and dedication. A few of the activities mentioned in this book are: circles, classes, intensive courses, giving and receiving messages, giving and receiving readings, researching lineages or ancestry, spending time in nature, spending time with animals, altar work, meditation, breathwork, creative work, reading books and articles, discussions with peers and mentors, and watching shows and movies.

I learned the phrase Gentle Consistency® from Dr. Shannon Ritchey, who started the exercise program I use called Evlo. She says, "Gentle Consistency® wins over intense inconsistency." One of her colleagues, Dr. Payton Busker, wrote about their philosophy with clear steps for developing an exercise routine. I've evolved them for mediumship:

Progressively overload: Work your way up from practicing alone to with one person to in groups. This also means starting with shorter sessions and slowly moving toward longer ones.

Find a schedule you can stick to most of the time: Develop a routine to work alone and meet with others, and use discernment for when you won't be able to show up.

Check in with yourself each time you start: This is inherently part of the connection process in mediumship, but check in before starting and adjust expectations accordingly.

Take at least two active rest days each week: It doesn't always need to be giving readings. Find time to talk about mediumship, read about it, watch *The X-Files*, sit and ponder existence, and all the activities in between.

Take an intentional break when needed: Time away often opens new ideas and can help break blocks that arise.

This isn't a competition, and nobody is watching except your poor, lonely ancestors waiting for you to finally help them—JUST JOKING. They're busy and fine.

---

1. What do you want to achieve with mediumship?
2. Are there other activities you must give up to make space for this one?
3. Which aspects of mediumship feel most important to you, and how can you align your practice to focus on them?

CHARTING YOUR COURSE

Give yourself a few moments to think of your mediumship journey, and allow your imagination to take you into the future. What do you hope you learn, experience, and try? Look back on your notes from the beginning of the book. How have your desires changed?

Here are some key aspects to consider when evaluating and developing the practice:

1. With whom do you want to practice mediumship?

   * On your own
     » With the body
     » In nature
     » In culture

   * With one person
     » Peers
     » Mentors
     » Sitters

   * In a group
     » Circles
     » Classes
     » Churches

4. How often do you want to practice mediumship?
     » Setting aside time
     » Incorporating into other activities

Forming Methods

5. Which formats do you want to explore with mediumship?

    - Discussions
    - Experiments
    - Experiences
    - Research

6. Which foundational skills for mediumship do you want to focus on?

    - Safety
    - Discernment
    - Presence
    - Embodiment
    - States of consciousness
    - Imagination
    - Relating
    - Creativity
    - Message work
    - Giving readings

CHAPTER 9

MEDIUMSHIP FOR CREATIVITY

In my earlier years of schooling and work, I rarely had more than two days in a row to choose how I might spend my time. But when I moved to Lily Dale, I often found myself alone, with nothing but a lot of time. My house projects occupied many of my daylight hours, and, because the Dale is a food desert, I cooked all my meals. Otherwise, I wasn't sure what to do with myself, and although I wanted to create, there was no stable outlet for it yet. Mediumship dropped into this void. Practicing connection with others offered me a little help in narrowing down my focus for creative work by handing over the question of "what should I make?" to my contacts.

Mediumship helped me build regularity into my practice by forcing me to keep trying repeatedly—a skill I could ultimately transfer to activities like drawing, singing, and playing the banjo. I started writing a novel the same way, writing one page per day. When I had nothing to write, I used mediumship to connect to a character or a place. After many years of feeling unmoored and unfocused, I finished the book in a hundred days—the first time I felt like I had truly completed an expression of my creativity.

The act of creating artifacts might be our species' finest gift. Ants build incredibly complex homes, monkeys use all sorts of tools, and fungi grow vast networks that traverse the planet. Humans produce a dizzying variety of crafts and art. Making things is an inherent part of our existence;

we all yearn to create. To the point that we threaten the very source of our materials, the planet, by making too many things. Living in a state of non-creation—whether through loss of inspiration, distraction, exhaustion, frustration, overconsumption, or any other common human struggle these days—is soul-crushing.

Creativity is one of the few things nearly everyone can agree is cool, acceptable, and good for us. This chapter is for everyone—not only professionals or those with training and experience—because we can all create. Imagine the creative process from beginning to end like a life where we are the vessels that bring it into being. We nurture our creations, offer them our time and energy, and give them form. We support our work in getting out into the world if needed or let it go if it's complete. There is no fixed time frame. The process could happen in five minutes, five years, five lifetimes. Keep returning to this: *I have something inside me that needs to get out.*

I suggest that both the inspiration and the support for creativity can come from beyond. If you sit and think about how an idea came to you from a past project, I am willing to wager the initial spark was not a rational process. Maybe it just appeared. You then did the honor of guiding it, feeding it, making it real, giving it a home, and allowing it to expand. This is a foundational idea for mediumship—something is coming to you from beyond, and you had better say it out loud.

Some Philosophy

I want to offer a theory for why mediumship and creativity are similar. Here are seven precepts that provide this foundation. They came to me during one of my early channeling sessions. See if reading them gives you a new way to approach creativity and a different mindset when you embark upon it. If the word "spirit" doesn't work for you, replace it with one you feel more drawn to, like the universe, God, or collective consciousness.

1. All creative work includes a human in connection to spirit—one's own or that of another.
2. The creative process moves the human through varying levels of consciousness and the spirit through various levels of physicality.
3. All creative work requires two skills: the technical ability (writing, painting, composition, etc.) and the connection ability. These two skills work in tandem.
4. Connection involves three steps: opening is an invitation, listening to the message is receiving, and using the message is translation. These can happen consciously or unconsciously for the human.
5. We can learn to control our connection and identify our sources to increase our conscious ability to work with spirit on our creative endeavors.
6. Connection with spirit is a dynamic activity that can be turned on, up, down, and off by the human at any time and throughout the creative process.
7. How much of oneself to include in the process is a personal choice. Reducing the distance between receiving and translating the message moves into deeper mediumship, which requires more connection with spirit and less interference from the human.

This is one way to articulate the mechanics of how we create. Note that creativity and creation are not singular acts but processes that follow a path like this:

1. Inspiration: I have an idea!
2. Articulation: I do something with that idea.
3. Assessment: I need another idea: return to step 1; this is what I wanted: move on to step 4.
4. Completion: I'm finished.

Mediumship for Creativity

Once you start the mediumship process, you will see that the middle is the same. We must have input and then transform that input somehow. This can happen over and over and over again. Then, at some point, we must finish. Without the closing of a mediumship connection or the completion of a creative project, we seep attention and energy through that open door. We can always open it again, but each creation must be allowed to leave us, to cut the umbilical cord and see if it can survive on its own.

Mediumship is helpful in creativity to find new and reliable sources of inspiration, wonder, and desire when we need them. Mediumship doesn't help directly with the articulation process—as noted in precept 3 above. That is another skill. We're also not working with *prophecy*, such as answers to questions like "Is this good enough?" or "Should I move on to the next project?" However, I have greatly improved my ability to answer those questions as I've developed my mediumship. The improved relationship with myself helps me use discernment and intuition, understand my truth, and live by it. I've developed the freedom and the courage to allow myself to emerge through my creativity, the confidence to know what I have done is good enough, the compassion to end projects, and the perspective to make the process precious and the outcome secondary.

We look at bringing together language from the two disciplines to understand the development of these skills—the control and sourcing of creative guidance. Dr. Judith Rochester taught me the different types of writing done by mediums. I have expanded the concepts she shares to include additional forms of creative work and provided a new axis to explain how the continuum of work has been created. On the horizontal axis, the level of human intellectuality moves from low to high. On the vertical axis, the engaged spirit's physicality level moves from low to high. The resultant types of activity are *physical mediumship* (far left: more spirit, less human), *mental mediumship* (middle: some spirit and some human), and regular creativity (far right: less spirit, more human).

Beyond

Types of Artistic Composition

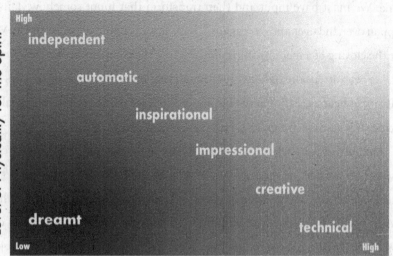

One way to understand how different relationships between humans and spirits produce artistic work.

ABOVE: Hilma af Klint in a photo taken during the 1910s. Photo © Fine Art Images/Bridgeman Images

The 2018 Guggenheim exhibition Hilma af Klint: *Paintings for the Future* was their most popular show *ever*. The public reception of af Klint's work not only rewrote the history of abstract art to include a woman for the first time, but it also brought mediumship for creativity into the public sphere. She worked with a group of four other women who called themselves "der Fem" ("the five"), as well as on her own, to bring in inspiration for art.

Jennifer Higgie's book *The Other Side* (Pegasus, 2024) gives an in-depth look at how af Klint, and

Mediumship for Creativity

many other visionary female artists, developed both artistic and mediumistic abilities. She didn't necessarily paint while connected to spirits but did automatic writing and drawing. She began attending séances in 1879 and first received messages in 1891—it took her eleven years to develop her mediumship abilities. Then it took another fifteen years to develop her relationship with spirit until 1906 when she got a "commission" from her spirit guide for the series of paintings that became her *Paintings for the Temple*, which took her until 1915 to complete. My understanding of her process puts her in the graph's "inspirational work" spot. She received instructions on what to make while connected to spirit(s), then made the work in a more regular creative state.

The most common association between mediumship and art is "automatic work." This is when the artist or medium is in active connection with a spirit and maintains the connection while creating the artwork. Automatic drawing, like that by Georgiana Houghton and Madge Gill, is done in a connected state. This work is often made with simpler materials such as pen, watercolor, and paper. Maintaining the altered state required for the connection becomes challenging if you're doing sculpture, needlepoint, or even working with paint and must keep choosing colors or changing brushes. However, it is possible with practice, especially if you're comfortable with your materials. The results tend to feel more wild, free, and imprecise.

Modern spirit artists do automatic drawing while working with a sitter, incorporating this real-time visual aspect into a mediumship session. Anne-Marie Bond is a spirit artist I saw

ABOVE: Madge Gill drawing on calico with black ink on her billiard table in her home in Upton Park, London, c. 1938.

demonstrate with another medium at Arthur Findlay College, where she drew as the medium gave a message to a sitter in a large audience. Watching a face emerge on the paper as the medium described the person added a captivating dimension to the message work. A friend who got one of the readings later showed me a photograph of her father, who Anne-Marie had drawn, and the resemblance was uncanny.

Independent work is rarely seen these days, but it occurs when the medium isn't even touching the materials, yet the spirits make a "precip-

TOP: Anne-Marie Bond, photo courtesy of the artist. **BOTTOM:** Helen and Edna Kelly, in Lily Dale, circa 1920. Photo courtesy of Ron Nagy, Lily Dale Museum.

itated" painting on their own. There is a collection of this type of art at the Maplewood Hotel in Lily Dale. The Bangs sisters were some of the most famous artists during the heyday of precipitated paintings. In a twist of fate, a photo of my great-grandmother, Edna Kelly, and her sister, Helen, was labeled as the Bangs sisters and spread throughout Spiritualist history books and museums. However, they were born thirty years later than May and Lizzie Bangs. Although none of my family were famous Spiritualists, somehow we got in the books anyway.

In creating a large composition, assume that the human/spirit team will move around in the different types of work. For example, there will be times when humans must engage in technical work alone, such as in the preparatory research phase of writing. Then the human may get into a flow and move into mediumship for a while, then back into editing or other technical work. While this may happen without the living human knowing or controlling the state, anyone can learn these skills to become aware of their connection and augment their creative process.

ABOVE: May and Lizzie Bangs, circa 1897. Photo courtesy of Ron Nagy, Lily Dale Museum.

Choosing a Purpose

We humans like to have a purpose. If you don't do anything for no reason, this is the time to start. But when you get tired of the ambiguity, take some time to work through why you want to do mediumship for creativity, both in the biggest sense and in the moment you sit down. The clearer our purpose is, the clearer we are. Conversely, when we have one thing going on way down deep, and we're saying something very different, we create an internal conflict that shows up in our work.

FIND A MEDIUMSHIP FOR A CREATIVITY PROJECT

Here's a meditation to find a project to work with as you practice mediumship.

You're in a little cave, and the space is widening. It's getting a little bit bigger. A light turns on. Now you can see around you, and you notice a table in front of you.

What's that table look like?

Imagine yourself approaching and sitting down at that table. Across from you is a TV. At first, it's a little TV, like an old-fashioned one that's small. So, you say, I need a much bigger one, maybe a projector. And that screen enlarges.

Now you can see a picture or a movie in great detail. And in that movie, you can see yourself sitting in front of a project. Maybe it's a piece of paper. Perhaps it's a kitchen counter, a computer, or a guitar. There's something that you can interact with and feel drawn toward.

As you watch yourself interact with that project in front of you, notice that you are doing something you've always wanted to do or enjoy doing—something that comes in the flow, that feels like it has ease, but it has energy, too. The you on the screen can keep with it, whatever it is doing there, while you at the table can ask questions.

And the first thing you ask yourself on the screen is, "What are you doing?" And without skipping a beat, you answer.

Why are you doing that?

Are you enjoying yourself?

What is it you're making?

Why are you making it?
How did you find this idea?
How will you know when it's done?
What else can you ask yourself? Then move to asking the project. Maybe you also want to ask the process. I'm going to leave you a few moments to ask.

When you've had a little bit of a conversation, thank yourself. Turn off the screen. When it goes away, notice there's something on the wall behind it. When you walk up close, you see a little message for yourself. There are a couple of words there. You move closer, read what it says, and take note.

Now you can turn back around and sit back at your table. Turn off the light in your little room. You take a few deep breaths and expand your focus into regular human size. Feel the rest of your body, remembering your mind, heart, and toes. You can expand your focus outside your physical body. Feel the boundaries of your skin when you breathe in, bringing your attention back into the middle of your chest by your heart and then allowing it to move up to your mind, to your brain, right behind your eyes, preparing yourself to open them. Come back to the external world when you're ready.

Motivations are complex. We have intentions, purpose, reasons, drives. They are conscious, subconscious, and unconscious. And they're constantly changing. It isn't easy to figure out why we do what we do. Getting into the practice of being upfront about why you're doing something—if only to yourself—takes time.

If you have no idea, make something up: What do you wish your purpose was? What is the coolest, most authentic, or noblest purpose you could imagine? Then find the negative: What do you hope is not your purpose? What would you be embarrassed to say is your purpose? Sometimes, it is more boring than that, like doing a thing because you hadn't thought of not doing it.

When asking "why," there is always the risk of getting stuck in analysis paralysis. Spending time unearthing our motivations can be fruitful but don't let the thinking keep you from the action. If this is a risk for you, set a timer and move on when it goes off. Leave solving the mystery for next time.

Choosing a Contact

Before opening ourselves up for connection, it helps to spend time deciding with whom to connect. The options are truly endless. We can change our minds at any point. In most cases, we won't have discernible "proof" that we've connected with whatever we've chosen. So why bother? Well, come back to the regular world for a moment. If I have a specific question, should I take an answer from anyone who offers a response? The comment section of anything public on the internet shows us why the answer is usually no. It is the same when we're in a transphysical realm. I like to pick a contact who can help with what I'm looking to do, and even if I specify nothing else, I ask that they support the purpose I've identified.

When deciding the best contact for the day or moment, we can get as specific as a particular person at a certain age or in an exact place. We can ask to connect to something vast, like the collective creative consciousness. We can connect to a project or a specific body part. This is a moment to think far and wide—even past a specific individual. Try working with their mother, house, year of birth, pen, hometown, rival, etc. This is also when I draw boundaries, protecting myself against those with whom I don't want to connect.

Choosing a Medium

The last thing to do before we get started is gather materials.

1. What do you have? Don't waste time getting something special—start with whatever you've got. Then make plans for more elaborate projects down the road.
2. What sounds fun? Pick something you want to work with so there's some energy behind it. Work toward the project you've been procrastinating or the ambitious new work that will push your edges by starting with something simple.
3. When do you plan to create within the mediumship process? If you're going to connect and then make, in other words, "inspirational" or "impressional" work, you can try any materials. If you go for "automatic work" or stay in the connection while you make, you will want something simple—a single mark-making device and paper, or simply the body and an instrument, finger paint, or clay. If you want to try "independent work," go with ink, watercolor, or other materials spirit can manipulate more easily.
4. What takes you out of connection? If you tend to get your mind mixed up in your process, try working with familiar materials that you have total fluency in (even typing on the computer) and foreign ones (that you don't have built-up expectations around). Find what loosens you up and gives you the freedom to explore.

5. What have you not done in a while? After doing this for some time, switch things up again. See how the connection changes and how you feel about the experience.

Writing is a natural way for me to connect and bring forward information, but it is also fraught with baggage around my expectations of the product. When Nika passed away, I was filled with grief. To cope, I would connect with her, receive an image, and sculpt it in clay. I found that the care and presence of making a little figure of her brought me great peace. When I first moved into my house here in Lily Dale, I'd get deep into connection in a closet and bring out melodies I'd record into my phone, then ask a musician friend to help me transcribe it into musical notation. I've seen people in my circles and classes make dances, sculptures, podcasts, paintings, funeral arrangements, personas for BDSM play, poems, music, and weavings.

Ritualizing Your Creativity

As much as you need to conceptualize the practice, ponder it with your mind. As much as you want to learn how it works, utilize the tools with your body. Find your balance between thinking of it and doing it. Too much thinking at the expense of doing so can leave you frustrated. Too much doing at the expense of thinking can leave you lost.

Here's the basic method for mediumship with creativity instead of a sitter.

1. Quiet.
2. Connect: confirm that the mind, body, spirit, and environment are appropriate for connecting.
   - Move attention to the space around the self, then to the self, the materials, and finally the contact point.

3. Ask.
    - Confirm consent with the contact.
    - Share intention with the contact.
    - Engage in dialogue.
4. Receive: notice what is happening in the mind and body while attention is at the contact point.
5. Translate.
    - Express the experience with your materials.
    - When approaching a creative decision, return to the contact or the materials for guidance.
6. Repeat.
7. Close.
    - Thank then withdraw attention from the contact, then the contact point, then the materials.
    - Bring all attention back to the self.

---

1. How have you been using mediumship in your creative practice all along? Where will it be most helpful to use mediumship when you create going forward?
2. What is your mediumship process? How do you need or want to adapt the process you've read to suit you?
3. Who inspires your creative work? Do you know what or who inspired those people?
4. What do you do when you feel creatively blocked? Get out your self-soothsayer deck and see if any of your tools for shifting neurological states help.

VISIONARY ART

Automatic writing, drawing, sculpting, or painting: Select a single implement and use your nondominant hand. Stay in the connection while you allow the implement to move across the page with as little physical or mental input from you as possible. This can be particularly interesting with watercolor or ink, which are very sensitive to manipulation, and with those with which you have direct contact, like finger paint or clay.

Indirect inspiration: Use something in the physical world to be your contact. Allow yourself to choose a tarot or oracle card, a passage from a book, a song, a photograph, food in the fridge, or anything else you have enough options to pick from randomly. Take a moment to connect with yourself and your intention, then ask which item wants to support you. Treat the contact as you would a person or spirit; ask questions, or let it guide you in writing or drawing. Allow your imagination to fill in the answers and wait for psychic information too. Make sure to disconnect and say thank you when you're done.

Creative decisions: Use your connection abilities in moments of creative decision-making. In addition to your aesthetics, sensibilities, practical considerations, and everything else you use to make creative choices, try allowing a contact you've chosen to make the call.

Start a project: Pick one thing to work on with the process and stick with it until it's done—something simple, in a form comfortable to you. Use your project or your creativity as a contact in sessions occasionally. Talk to it about how it wants to be expressed and your relationship. I have done that with this book, returning to it repeatedly as not merely an idea or a creation but a wise being with its own experience and desires.

Mediumship for Creativity

Form a creativity circle: When I had one, we met on the same day and time each week with the following format:

* Fifteen minutes or so of chatting, sharing anecdotes and updates on our projects and materials.

* Five minutes or so of quieting, settling in, and guided meditation into a receptive state of being.

* Ten to fifteen minutes of readings, card pulls, or other inspirational input. I'd often read aloud for the group from a few short sources, like poems, which would provide input to our creative side, or a scientific paper or article to provide fodder for our intellectual side.

* Forty-five minutes of art-making. I'd prepare a playlist with no vocal elements for us to listen to. You can find a few of them on the NT2TD website.

* Thirty minutes of sharing afterward. Seeing the synchronicities in what we made was so enlivening.

CHAPTER 10

DEVELOPMENT CIRCLES

The first message I gave was in Dr. Judith Rochester's Friday night community mediumship class in January 2018. At that point, I had been reading tarot for nearly fifteen years, but tarot involves material objects, and the way I did readings, the sitter and I had the shared experience of looking at the cards. In mediumship, the sitter cannot see what I see, only what I describe to them. This was a significant shift that made me unsure of myself.

There were probably twenty people at the *development circle*, more women than men, more older folks than young, all white, from every walk of life in western New York. Judith started with a talk to explain the mediumship concept of the evening, followed by a guided meditation. The similarity to journeying practices immediately struck me. I'd been doing that for years—except this meditation (and most I've encountered with mediums) goes up into the heavens instead of down into the ground.

Afterward, we paired off to try the technique she had described. I was shocked. Less than thirty minutes after I first heard a description of mediumship and how to do it, I was expected to give someone a "message from spirit." I asked my partner, a man I see around town to this day, to go first. I don't remember what he told me, but I can still see the image I attempted to give him as a message.

I saw a desk in an upstairs room in a house like mine. One of those green glass-shaded lamps of gold or bronze sat on the desk like a banker might have. The lamp shone, and without much other light in the room. That's it. I describe it to him. He had no idea what I was talking about. I was not surprised. Without confirmation that what I said made sense, I shrugged my shoulders and apologized unnecessarily, and we sat there awkwardly until it was time to go back to the main group.

It was not a promising start, but I had nothing to do other than fix my house and knew nobody within a few hours' drive beside my uncle Gary, who made me do farm chores when I visited. (Okay, "made" is a bit of an overstatement—I loved this. Of all the jobs I've ever had, my favorites were baking chicken pot pies for him and tapping maple trees for syrup for his neighbor.)

Judith's class was a two-minute walk from my house, and nothing else was, so I kept going. It took a few weeks to give my first message that someone could understand. This time it wasn't in partners, but around a whole circle. I told a woman that I saw her son was getting married and wanted to reach out and tell her. I winced as I waited to hear if she could accept the message. I was nervous because it didn't make sense—if the message was coming from a spirit, they couldn't be having a wedding the woman could attend. It turns out her son was alive but estranged. Through tears, she said the message signified it was time to get in touch.

Those who have learned a second language will have a leg up in learning mediumship because both require pushing past the fear of sounding wrong. At some point, we must get the words out before we feel ready. Only when we take that leap do we get the opportunity to get it right as well. This makes the learning environments of circles, practice readings and messages, and classes helpful for mediumship.

I knew what I was saying to the woman in that message didn't make sense, but Judith and the rest of the circle were all there without expectations, and I felt I could say the words. And the woman had the space to respond with her true reaction, explaining what the information meant, regardless of whether I was correct. For the first time I could match the experience of receiving information for someone with their interpretation. This real-time feedback from a sitter is invaluable. It teaches us what connection feels like when they validate and correct the content we bring through. This is still true for someone saying they don't understand what you've said—with enough experience of yeses and nos, we can learn the feeling of a strong connection.

The actual act of mediumship, the relating, starts with the medium and their contact. At some point, some may want to include other living humans in the process. Practicing with fellow student mediums is important in the early stages of mediumship development—it ensures every message is an exchange. This even power dynamic reduces the pressure on the medium, gives space and time to figure out mechanics, and allows a sitter to provide honest feedback. We are prone to poorly delivering incorrect information when first starting. Another medium in training knows that and will take readings with a grain of salt while being empathetic to the challenges of learning this work.

Mediumship classes should include a reasonable amount of time to practice with fellow students and demonstrations by the teacher; both are great ways to see how other people work. Circles and development groups typically have less teaching time and instead focus on practice. Look for experiences that allow you to give one-on-one readings to another person with time for feedback, such as in pairs or breakout rooms, and within a group, to feel what it is like to have an audience.

Keeping out of the rational mind and personal interests is more accessible with strangers than with people we know. I found a curve in my development where I first gave messages to people closest to me. They were the only ones I had the guts to try this with outside class. As I practiced, I arrived at a place where I only wanted to work with strangers, preferably by phone, so I could not see them. I wanted as little information as possible from any non-psychic source. After years of learning better boundaries, mediumship skills, and the ability to articulate when something comes from me, I love to read for my friends and family again.

Message Work

Most people consider mediumship to be the sharing of messages from the departed. I hope it is apparent that this can also be done with any combination of sources and contacts. A message is a short bit of content, typically two to ten minutes' worth, that the medium says aloud (although it could be written) for a specific sitter.

In Spiritualist mediumship, message work can be done in a one-on-one setting, such as a medium's reading room, a church event, or publicly, as a demonstration in front of an audience. Several demonstrations are held daily throughout the season in Lily Dale and Spiritualist church services worldwide. They are also prominently featured on TV shows and at celebrity medium events. Public demonstration, also called *platform mediumship*, is an advanced skill that requires mastering small-group and one-on-one messages first, so we will focus on those for now.

The medium connects to a single spirit (usually there is time for only one, but this isn't a hard and fast rule) for a single sitter (again, it could be for a couple or small group).

A student's first messages should be done in pairs so they do not need to decide to whom to bring a message. Then we can branch out to a circle, where we must decide with whom to connect for a message. In Spiritualist-style group message work, two approaches are common: spirit first or sitter first. These are sometimes called British-style and American-style mediumship, respectively. In British style, the medium connects to the spirit first, and information is shared to the group, slowly narrowing down the potential sitter from the audience until enough information has come through to decide who the sitter should be. Then the message is shared. In American style, the medium chooses a sitter first, asks if they'd like a message, and if the sitter says yes, the evidence is given until the sitter can identify the spirit. Then the message is given.

We will discuss the specifics of this form of mediumship, with its protocols and expectations, as I have found these clear and relatively widespread rules create a bounded space conducive to learning. This is, however, a limited view of what is possible. If we can expand the idea of a contact, we can also expand the concept of a message. When rules are less prescribed, or when in doubt, act as though you're dealing with a living person that everyone acknowledges is there.

Choosing a Sitter

If American-style mediumship is expected in the setting, you'll have to start the message by asking a specific living human if you can work with them. You can do this any way you want and try something different every time in the beginning. I like to look at each person and then close my eyes and feel where my energy drifts. I will then go to the person the energy leads me toward.

I have friends who see a light or extra energy around a person and will start with them as their sitter. You can just pick the person you want to talk to. Generally, allow yourself to follow your natural inclinations. If nothing comes to you, relax and let yourself know what you want from this message: a chance to practice getting evidence through songs, for example. The more specific, the better. Then forget your intention and listen for a moment.

Choosing a Spirit

You can always start by first seeing what spirit is around, getting a connection going with them, and asking them to whom they want to speak. If the situation requires British-style mediumship, you will have to do this, and protocol will dictate if you may directly identify the sitter right away, even if you know who it is. I usually have only one spirit at a time, so if I go spirit-first, it is merely a matter of order, not of deciding. If you have a few to choose from, use the same techniques discussed above for a sitter, and ask the contact why they want to give a message. This will help to see who you have a good rapport with or find interesting.

Considerations for Contacts Other than Dead People

When you work with spirits that a sitter knows, they will have an existing relationship so the contact can give you information about the sitter. If you work with guides or nonhuman contacts such as deities, extraterrestrials, or elementals, they may not have connected to your sitter. You must avoid creating a situation where you invite the contact to connect with the sitter without their consent. Instead maintain your connection with the contact and ask them for information on the sitter's behalf.

Permission

I believe a medium must get verbal consent to give a message—just like you wouldn't walk up to a stranger and start telling them things. If you have multiple potential sitters, such as in a circle, the medium will also need to identify for whom the message is intended. If names are unknown, you will have to describe the person. If you are in physical space, try to use location. If that is not possible, use descriptors of the person's clothing rather than their physical features. It is very uncomfortable to hear mediums accidentally call someone old or the wrong gender. I avoid all that with a simple "Can I come to you in the third row with the light blue polo shirt?" Even if it is only you and the sitter, you will want to ask and get an affirmative response before starting; this can be as simple as "May I begin?"

Evidence of the Spirit

This is the information the spirit gives you so the sitter can identify them. This can be anything—like a living person could say anything. I've seen many different lists of appropriate evidence. The advice I learned from all my mediumship teachers is to keep track of what type of information you get, ask for new categories, and strengthen what works. I usually start a message by saying how the spirit feels to me. Once that connection is made, I will get some visual data. We're looking for data that describes a person, their life, or their relationship to the sitter. Evidence used to prove the spirit is present is less engaging than evidence that is part of the story. Each piece of data can give the sitter and the medium a clue into what the spirit is here to share. They've come to tell the sitter something. They could bring in any information—so why have they shown you exactly what they have chosen? Here are some common categories:

Intrinsic traits
- Appearance and conditions
- Personality and behaviors
- Speech and movement patterns

External factors
- Background
- Living situations and important locations
- Relationships

Life and death experiences
- Skills and abilities
- Interests, careers, and hobbies
- Memorable events
- Memories with the sitter
- Habits and routines
- Strengths and weaknesses

Philosophy and outlook
- Goals and aspirations
- Values and beliefs
- Impact on others
- Legacy

Here's an example of identifying a spirit in a reading. In this case, I start by explaining how I experienced the connection, which showed me how the spirit died. Then, I delve into his personality traits, followed by a very brief physical description. This is from a reading with a mother and her two adult daughters.

A quick note on the reading examples: these transcripts come from readings I've given and recorded. These sessions were given for free, with the sitter agreeing that the transcripts could be anonymized and used in the book. Each one was approved by the sitter and edited for clarity.

ME: So when I connect with you, I feel there's a man here, and he's quite far away. He would have passed a while back, and when he passed, he sort of went off. It feels like he passed quite quickly, or it would be more unexpectedly than quickly. It came out of nowhere. It feels like an illness, though, not an accident.

He was a person who searched for things and answers, would look into things very deeply, and had a deep well of knowledge. His approach to life was focused on the depths of things. It does feel like he was an intellectual who liked to learn and understand things very deeply.

I feel like he wore glasses. When he passed, he was similar in age to the aunt we talked to before—middle-aged, maybe in his fifties or something like that. Is this somebody you recognize from this information?

SITTER 1: I mean, it sounds very much like Dad to me. Middle age, unexpected. He did have a heart condition that was the cause of death, and he was forty-five.

ME: And was he an intellectually curious kind of person?

[I brought back this specific question because it was the most essential part of how I felt him.]

SITTER 1: My memories of it is yes. The thing of mastery really resonated with me in terms of craft and building skills. He was a guitarist, so from my experience, that was witnessing sort of practice, relentless practice, night after night. I feel that Mom, you could probably speak more to an intellectual sort of identity, but that really sounds familiar to me. And he did wear glasses.

SITTER 2: Yeah, mostly glasses for reading. Yeah, yeah. Middle-aged. Yeah.

[If the sitters have correctly identified the spirit, the spirit will typically let me know with emotional upwelling or goose bumps; the former happened here.]
ME: Okay. As you're talking about him, it feels like we are talking about the same person. And he likes to come in very close now and be near all of you. So, this is Sitter 1 and 3, your father, and Sitter 2, your husband?
SITTER 2: Yep.

Evidence of the Sitter

Once the spirit has been identified, I like to give information from the spirit about the sitter. If the evidence for the sitter is presented with a strong spirit connection, it helps to set the stage for the message and ensure that I have connected well to the spirit and the sitter's wants and needs.

This information can fall into the same categories listed above, and the point is to show that both you and the spirit have tuned into what the sitter came for. It often shows up as relating the evidence given for the spirit to corresponding evidence for the sitter. If this is done without a solid spirit connection, it is typically considered psychic work rather than mediumship. Sitters may appreciate it regardless of where the information came from; be upfront about it.

This example continues from the earlier reading, where the spirit wanted to discuss one of the sitters' children. I start by verifying that what I see from the spirit is correct.

ME: Do one of you, or maybe both of you, have children?
SITTER 1: Mm. I do. Yeah.
ME: Did you have the children after he passed?
SITTER 1: Yeah.
ME: Okay. So, [your father] is enjoying being able to watch them grow up and watch you all together as well. Is the older one a boy?
SITTER 1: Yeah.

Development Circles

ME: So, he definitely feels this kindred feeling with him, especially. Is he old enough to read yet?

SITTER 1: He's just starting to.

ME: Okay. It feels like that he's quite excited about that. And there are certain books that he hopes you read to him. He feels very excited about the prospect of him becoming a reader. You know, he has all these things he hopes he's going to do and learn about, and he's very excited, watching him grow up. And that's not to say he's not excited about your other—you have two children?

SITTER 1: I do, yeah.

Here's another example from a different reading where the sitter's father came in to share traits he had in common with the sitter. This was an experienced sitter, so I explained more context to her with the information.

ME: He uses many of these really physical metaphors when sharing things. So, it's not many words, but he's showing me things in the physical world as metaphors. I'm just sharing that because it's really interesting. I haven't had somebody talk or communicate like that. Is that how he talked or thought?

SITTER: He didn't talk a lot.

ME: Okay. Maybe that's why I feel like he must have had a lot going on in his mind, and he saw the world and how everything fits together in this way. That is very difficult to communicate in words. I don't even know what it is he's showing me—these interlocking things. I want to say that he's got a very visual mind. Do you think like that, too?

SITTER: I don't talk much but have a very active mind.

ME: I wonder if that's why he's sharing this a little bit: to connect and share how things are for him. There's so much he's got going on, and only this tiny bit makes it into words. It's like he can see how everything works. He's saying you see how people work, how they fit together, and how things move by people interacting and that

this is an incredible way of understanding the world. Does that make sense to you?
SITTER: Yeah.

The Message Itself

There must be a *reason* for connecting with the spirit. I've received readings where the medium only brings through evidence, which is very dull. People want to hear something from the spirit regarding their current life. Many spirits will want to say they're sorry, tell the sitter they love them, share how much they miss them, and let them know they are okay. These sentiments aren't always enough on their own. Further information for the sitter to overcome challenges or celebrate successes can create an empowering and meaningful message. Consider the main categories of a person's life (relationships, money, health, and purpose are common requests) and see if there isn't something the spirit has to say concerning one or more of them.

Here's part of a message from a third reading where two male spirits came through for a sitter.

ME: There's a reason you have that skill. You experienced it throughout all this time, and you probably didn't even know when you were younger that it was happening, but you learned to read them or understand them. Maybe you don't necessarily recall it with those two grandfathers, but they say it was around many other people. They want to say how important and rare it is and make it explicit that this work is difficult and valued.

They're like, everybody has something to say, and they're not always going to say it, but giving them the space to express it in whatever way they can means a lot. And they are mainly talking about expressing it through behavior—how they act. That's how they communicated. And the one talks about it more standoffishly, like, less one-to-one communication, but more in acting. Like, in. Sorry. In. In working.

[It took me a moment to understand what the second spirit was saying.]

The only way he communicated was by doing something for somebody and then by not doing—by leaving and not doing anything. Does this make sense? Do you have questions about it?

[I paused to ask because it wasn't apparent to me.]

SITTER: I'm still . . . I'm processing it, but yeah, it totally makes sense. It also kind of feels like one is justifying himself. I mean, the family has talked many times about my grandfather and how he left. And so, I think it's interesting what you're saying. That this is something that's being brought up. I was one of the last people to see him before he passed away, and so I have a completely different idea of the leaving than the rest of the family does.

Showing and Telling

Like with any communication, you can give all this information to the sitter through showing or telling. You don't have to choose one and never do the other; you may choose each time, with each piece of information, if you want. I typically deliver all my messages as a play-by-play, with as little interpretation as possible. I will move into the first person (speaking as the spirit) when I have a strong connection. If I interpret something, I let the sitter know what I'm doing, and I do it after I've given the information as I've received it. It empowers the sitter to come to their own conclusions and keeps me out of it a little more. I also occasionally support connecting with the dead directly for sitters to use independently. Here's an example from the earlier reading with the three women.

SITTER 1: I have a question about the best ways for us to connect with him or how best to recognize when he is attempting to connect with us—things for us to be aware of, pay attention to, or see specifically.
ME: It feels like he sometimes comes in as almost like a breath of air because of his connection with the ocean and his love for that feeling of wind in his hair and face.

It feels like you sometimes have that feeling of something whooshing by. And that might be a physical indicator for you. He also would be fine with any sort of light . . . he says light ritual, where you come together and bring something of his, or especially going out to the ocean and bringing something, or having a few moments where you talk about him or recall memories and just having some kind of regular, maybe on a . . . what did you say when you booked this? It was his birthday.

[A memory of my own came up, so I called it out as such.]

SITTER 1: Yeah. Today.

ME: Okay. It's like, happy birthday. Happy birthday! He likes this.

[Here the emotion of the birthday brought a switch to the first person from the spirit's perspective.]

I like that. Can we maybe celebrate again?

[Then I switch back.]

Bring maybe the food he likes or do something he would have liked to do and spend time sharing memories. That kind of thing would feel special to him. Also, when you play the music. He says that he sort of pops in with memories.

[Now I want to tell them more from the perspective of the living, so I switch to first person from my perspective.]

And then I, Tiffany, will say, I feel like whenever that happens, when a memory pops in, that's when they're coming. I don't get a lot of physical reminders. It happens occasionally with some of my loved ones; they pop into my head, and then I take a moment to just . . . I wouldn't quite say it's fully talking to them, but you know, have a little bit of a back and forth in my mind or relish the memory for a little bit.

[Now back to the spirit.]

And he's saying that he does both.

SITTER 2: Yeah, he showed up in a yoga class with me and one of my friends that he knew. She was teaching the class. There were twelve or fifteen of us in the room, and he was there. He would talk to both of us. Well, she saw him. He and

I were talking, and she saw us talking. That was very... yeah. First time ever. That had happened years ago.

Style and Grace

You will develop your style with a tone or approach that builds rapport with your sitters. Even short messages are personal and take a measure of vulnerability to receive. This isn't a casual encounter, which must be considered in your delivery. The medium is entrusted not to harm the sitter; that is your job, no matter what. Some say that all messages must be positive, and while positivity can quickly turn toxic without a dose of reality, message work often skirts that boundary very closely. Some say that they work to share the truth—not maintain comfort. When relaying personal information to a sitter, we must decide why we engage in the activity and develop a manner conducive to that approach. Kindness, hope, and respect are foundational for every case. From there, you can choose for yourself.

Limits

A few items are generally considered off-limits in psychic work. Some people decide never to give advice; others offer advice if the sitter asks for it or affirms directly that they would like it. In addition to any content that would violate your purpose and ethics, it is unwise to do so much as confirm information surrounding births or deaths. Any advice-giving needs consideration, but information on legal, health, or money matters can create liability issues. Leave that out and remind the sitter you are not a lawyer, doctor, financial advisor, etc. You may have precise details regarding these things, and the sitter may want to hear them, but be very sure before you deliver that message.

Take a Moment

While giving a message, I pause if I get stuck, a sitter doesn't understand what I'm saying, or nothing is coming through. I take a moment to breathe, feel my body, and ask the spirit (or, if I don't have one yet, my gatekeeper) to help me. I ask them to be more straightforward if I can't understand what they're saying. If the sitter doesn't understand, I ask the spirit what they want the sitter to know and then take a moment to listen. If I feel like I'm taking a long time, I tell the sitter I need a moment. This slows the process and relieves some pressure that builds up when we get nervous or uncomfortable. It happens to me often, both in mediumship and outside; it is normal and part of life.

Start (or Join) a Development Circle

A development circle is a small group gathering for practicing mediumship skills. In traditional Spiritualist mediumship development, the circle was the primary way of learning how to talk to the dead. They had elaborate protocols regarding who could be in them, when they met, what people could wear, and how they ordered themselves in the circle. Closer to current times, my teacher Elaine Thomas learned in a circle without so much explicit protocol, but more like a church setting. The only way to get better without much instruction was to sit there and try it.

Nowadays there are a variety of mediumship development circles. They often mix skill levels; everyone is expected to act as both medium and sitter. This is opposed to a séance ("session" in French but typically refers to physical mediumship only), *gallery readings,* or demonstration, where only a single medium works and everyone else is a sitter. It also differs from a class where a teacher provides instruction and guidance. In the circle, we might help each other to bring a message through, but there isn't always a single person designated as the instructor.

This way, development circles are free from a hierarchy between sitter and medium or teacher and student. A strong circle provides a free, open, yet supportive environment to learn, explore, and develop skills. There are resources at the end of this book for finding an existing development circle. If you want to start your own, here are some elements to consider.

Membership

It takes time to find people for a circle. Once you have a few, agree with the group on guidelines and let new people know them when they join. Flexibility around who comes can strengthen the circle if everyone follows the same rules. Some people run closed circles, meaning only those who start the circle can participate, except under certain circumstances or at certain times. Some open their circles to anyone, and some sit in between, where you need to know someone or be invited to join. While the traditional format of keeping the same people over time creates stronger bonds between the mediums, having new folks with unique capabilities and spirit networks can enhance everyone's growth.

Regularity

You will want to get to know people in your circle. In the olden days, people would meet weekly without missing a session for *years*. You might not be able to require people to come to every meeting, but you will need a large enough group so that at least three people show up to each session. My circle is monthly. That's the minimum you'll need to keep the living human relationships going. It took us three years before we had a jaw-dropping circle meeting once a month. Weekly sessions will progress faster.

Leadership

Someone will need to hold the space for the group by watching time, managing logistics, and sending invitations. This does not need to be the same person each time or doing all the aspects of circle management. But if that's the case, consider providing that person with funds for their efforts. Unless the leader is also teaching, it can be a nominal amount. Development circles are meant to be communal, but you will need a certain level of confidence to get there, so it doesn't hurt to join a circle led by a teacher in the beginning so you can get comfortable.

Location

A video conferencing link that lets everyone join even if the account holder isn't there and ideally doesn't end the meeting after forty minutes will work. If you are lucky enough to meet in person, ensure people aren't coming or going through the space. Consider the temperature, lighting, smells, and sounds in the location and how they might affect the concentration of the group.

Focus

Living humans need to have conversations at the beginning or end to get to know each other. However, the line between chatting and giving messages must be well delineated. Someone can watch over the tenor of the group to move from conversation into messages and vice versa by verbally asking the group if they are ready to shift gears. During messages, a sitter might respond to a medium's feedback request, but too much discussion can shift the energy. Instead, save time after for people to talk through their experiences.

Balance

Like any communal event, speaking time should stay balanced throughout the group. Once you've given a message, wait until everyone else has had a turn before providing another one. This isn't a hard and fast rule, but quiet time is necessary—no need to fill the silence. The same goes for the chatting part: if you or someone else talks significantly more than everyone else, it isn't a circle. Ask them privately to pay more attention to the balance among the group.

Structure

Decide on the structure of your circle before you start, and periodically discuss it to see if members would like changes. My circle begins with a discussion of how mediumship shows up in our lives, and then, when we're ready, I lead us in a short meditation. I open the circle, and we give messages until we've gone for an hour and a half. Sometimes it's an hour of talking and a half hour of messages, and sometimes the other way around. You may want to consider longer meditations and breaking into pairs to practice one-on-one readings.

Protocol

Any existing circle you join will have a protocol. Don't be afraid to ask what it is. There is no universal right or wrong here—whatever feels supportive for the group. Some circles don't allow people to build on each other's messages, for example, which means that even if you can fill in more details for a message that another medium gives, you'll need to keep it to yourself. Some only allow communication with the dead, while others allow a wider variety of contacts. Some allow open messages to the whole circle, and some do not. In all cases, it is helpful for everyone to verbally communicate boundaries. Verbally open the circle, verbally close it. Verbally ask each other before bringing through a message: "May I come to you, [name]?" or "[name], would you like a message?" Verbally accept or decline an offer for a message. Verbally end your message when you finish with "That's it" or "I'll leave that with you."

Discretion

It is generally expected that members of a circle will not discuss the happenings of a circle to nonmembers unless otherwise agreed upon. If you want to share your experience giving or receiving a message with someone who was not present, consider not mentioning identifying information unless you have permission. While some early Spiritualists' detailed records of every message in their circles have been historically significant, only one of the many circles I have joined records and transcribes our sessions.

OPENING AND CLOSING A CIRCLE

Here's a meditation and opening to adapt to your circle. You will want to verbally invite the connection you seek. A few customizations to consider are:

- The specific being(s) or types of beings you wish to call in
- The boundaries of what types of information or guidance you seek
- The purpose of your connection
- How you want to communicate (images, feelings, words, etc.)

As we start to settle in, notice your breathing. Begin to close your eyes when you feel ready. Move your body to find a posture that allows for good blood flow and breath. Start connecting to your body, noticing how you are today, your energetic state, and your thoughts and feelings swirling inside. Begin to relax into our circle and this time for practice. Lengthen your breath, allow it to go deeply into your belly, and fully exhale all your air out.

When you feel you have a strong connection with your being, energetically connect with everyone else here tonight. Call to mind those present, imagining an energetic connection between us. As we do this, we connect into not only a circle but a web, creating a container for our learning and growth. As we make this container, we ask that only those who can safely speak to us in ways we can understand join in. We hold our circle against those who may harm ourselves or others.

As we feel strong in our interconnectedness, we reach out to the spirit realm, letting our loved ones, teachers, protectors, and guides know we are here to connect. We ask them to bring us information that applies to our lives right now, words for the healing and empowerment of this group and the wider world, and support for our mediumship development.

With that, I open the circle. Please speak as you feel moved.

After we have all given messages, we are at time, or if it has been silent for a while, I will ask if everyone is ready, then close the circle with something like this:

With that, we close the circle, taking a moment to call our energy back from the spirit realm into the circle. We thank all who came to us today and brought their presence into this time and place. We acknowledge that the connection between our realms is ever stronger each time we access it and that it is there for us the next time we open it. We close the connection for now.

Then we withdraw our energy from the circle and thank everyone for showing up, bringing what they could, and sharing with each other.

As we draw our energy back fully inside ourselves, sitting deeply into our bodies, we take a moment to thank our beings for their presence and dedication to this work, which is essential to our growth and that of the world.

Tell a Friend

Mediumship can feel lonely. It takes you out of this world, in a way, and not everyone understands that. I'm in one of the most densely medium-populated places in the world, so it is normal at home. But it is not normal anywhere else.

I have slowly, slowly, over the years, come "out of the closet." You can go your whole life not telling anyone you're a medium, or you can tell everyone the first time you meet them. You will probably do something in the infinite space between. I don't have any rules for who I tell; I take it on a purely case-by-case basis. I've told potential employers in job interviews but haven't told my biological father.

Talking about mediumship is for more than practice. We find someone to talk to about our interests and experiences, too. Finding the right person may take some time, or you may explore this with a friend from the beginning. You may need to think carefully about it, or it may tumble out of your mouth and onto understanding ears. I have been surprised over and over who is interested in mediumship. Sometimes the topic has emerged in a conversation and I have been terrified, only to find that the person is not assuming anything negative but is merely curious about the whole thing.

The ideal person will not only want to extract information from you. There is a concept in some spiritual traditions that reminds students to be careful to whom they tell their spiritual activities because it can diminish spiritual power. There is something to this. People sometimes ask me question after question, as if learning from me will give them what I've acquired with time and practice. There is a fine line for the asker between wanting to learn and wanting to acquire with speed and ease. There is a fine line for the answerer between wanting to share and wanting to acquire the power of being the person who is asked.

The people to talk with about mediumship are those who care for you more than mediumship. They will want to know how it makes you feel and how it has changed your life. They might have tough questions to keep you safe and ensure you're not falling prey to anything "culty" or losing your sense of reality. Try not to bristle at their questions; thank them for checking that you're maintaining your integrity. They may or may not care at all about mediumship itself. If you have these people in your life, treasure them. I hope they share with you what brings them sparks of life.

If you don't have these people, the time may have arrived to cultivate relationships with good old-fashioned strangers on the internet. A development circle is meant not only to give you space to practice mediumship and receive messages from other mediums. It is a place for sharing experiences outside the circle and checking on each other. Building rapport and trust with people you meet occasionally online takes time, but it can be rewarding.

1. Whom might you talk to about your interests and experiences in mediumship? With whom do you feel safe sharing this part of yourself? With whom are you not ready to talk about mediumship?
2. What kind of circle feels right for you? Should you also take classes?
3. What is your mediumship process now that you're working with others? How do you need or want to adapt the process you've developed?
4. Go back to your support list from Chapter 3 with people for when you need help, and update it if needed.

EXPANDING THE CIRCLE

Circles can be for any part of the mediumship process, not only messages. Healing, meditation, creativity, imagination, co-regulation, or anything else you want to practice with others can benefit from creating a regular meeting. They also don't have to be recurring. I've done a few different one-time circles:

* **Mourning circle:** As my grandmother Joan was preparing for her transition (a common way Spiritualists refer to death), my mom, Molly, and I held a little circle to ease the process and help us manage our grief. We gathered photos from all different times of her life, lit candles, and shared memories. We asked our close family who couldn't be in person with us to spend a few moments in prayerful repose at the same time. We then asked some of the most influential people in Joan's life who had already passed to guide her to the other side.

* **Birthday party séance for change:** I had a great time inviting my friends and family to an online circle for my birthday right before the 2020 election. I invited people who usually wouldn't be involved in mediumship but said yes as a gift to me. Here is the text of the invitation:

  We will gather (virtually) on the evening of October 8 (my actual birthday) to celebrate and do a little Libra-time experiment in freedom and justice for all.

  Join me at 9 p.m. ET / 6 p.m. PT. You have homework, though: before that night, and regardless of whether you can attend, please spend a few moments thinking about (aka psychically inviting) a dead person who might be able to help us out. A relative, activist, former president, or whoever you believe will help us in our noble mission. Someone you feel you know well enough to be able to say a few words from their perspective.

* **A séance for dead projects:** There's only one kind of resurrection I'm into: the resurrection of a beloved project long dead. Find a few friends to hold a séance to connect with the projects you've lost along the way. Bring a project you would like to work on again, maybe some that have slipped through your fingers or met frustrating blockages. Each person can bring in their project, have a conversation out loud with the project, and ask if it wants to come back to life, what needs to change or happen for it to come, and why it left or failed the first time around. Make agreements in the presence of your friends about what you are or are not willing to do if the project comes back. If you make promises to a resurrected project, watch out if you forget it again! Nothing like a project scorned—twice.

Listen to Jessica Lanyadoo's *Ghost of a Podcast*, particularly an episode where she gives a reading and brings through the dead. Jessica is an astrologist, psychic medium, and animal communicator with decades of experience giving readings with strong, consistent ethics and skills. As you listen, notice how she uses questions during the reading, how she prefaces advice, and her balancing of comfort and truth.

Now that you are beginning to develop your process, make a pie chart with the unique skills and attributes that contribute to your mediumship.

This is also a good time to reconsider your list of boundaries from Chapter 3. Looking back on that section, what new experiences have you had that require changes to your boundaries?

CHAPTER 11

OFFERING READINGS

By the summer between the first and second year of the Fellowships program, I had given hundreds of messages and readings to classmates, friends, community members at church events, and strangers from Craigslist. By this time, I had clients hang up on me when I wouldn't connect into their (living) ex-boyfriends. I had sitters *not* hang up after our time had ended, asking question after question. I had people not show up to our appointments, and then other people try to book readings week after week. Folks came to me brokenhearted after losing children or parents or spouses, fixated on trivial matters they couldn't control, or lost and adrift in their lives. I had been giving (free) mediumship readings for a *year.* When classes stopped for the season, I had more time for everything to seep in, and I was overwhelmed with the weight of it all. No individual had acted egregiously, but cumulatively, it was a *lot*. I had always suspected that giving readings full-time would not work for me, and this first year seemed to have proven that.

I went to Elaine Thomas and told her I wouldn't continue with the course. She said something very similar to what my undergraduate thesis advisor told me when I couldn't decide whether I wanted to be an artist or a scientist: some people can follow a well-defined path to a career that is unique to them but similar to others. Some people can't. In my application to Fellowships, I mentioned my desire to work with creativity and mediumship. Elaine assured me that just because most of my classmates would go on to give readings as their job, like

Offering Readings

most of my neighbors already had, I didn't have to. She also reminded me that learning to do readings accurately and ethically is a profound act of service that helps us care for ourselves as we care for others. I saw how my mind, wanting to make sense of mediumship, was getting in the way of my heart, curious to connect. I returned for the program's second year and graduated in late 2020.

Mediumship readings are extended, one-on-one messages. They are a form of care work. One person takes time out of their life to focus on another person's needs. It is a beautiful and essential act to care for another. It is rare and special. It is *work*. Work denotes responsibility and asks for reciprocation. Giving readings requires learning a new skill set on top of mediumship: providing one-on-one care.

This is serious. Although mediumship readings can feel lighthearted and full of laughter and joy, they often bring tears and catharsis. A good reading brings resolution to a problem, which is mentally and emotionally taxing for both people. And if someone has a problem they're coming to a stranger for, it is likely significant. On the other hand, you may want to work with another medium to receive this kind of care, for which this chapter should prepare you. If you want to do care work, this chapter will be only one step in a long journey.

Even if you never accept money for your work, one-on-one readings require training, ethics, and practice in mediumship and working with people. And if you accept money for your work, you also run a business, which requires accounting, marketing, logistics, sales, and customer service.

I want to point out the rather obvious but obscured point that I do not recommend mediumship as a preferred method of offering care. Most people, most of the time, are better off getting our attention than getting a reading. How often do you spend half an hour totally focusing on a loved one? With every bit of your attention on them the whole time? Who does that for you? If mediumship becomes your way to provide that to people as it has for me, this chapter will give you a peek into what that entails. As always, I offer what works for me based on my training and experience.

I am fascinated by how much the sitter brings to the table with a reading, even if they have never had one. Somewhere in the movies, on TV, or in the story of a friend—however they came to it—people have something in mind when they hire a medium. My process here reflects my desire to provide healing and expansion for my sitters that matches the cultural expectations of this day and age. I hope some of these expectations shift over time because providing mediumship readings is hard. Unrealistic expectations from ourselves or our sitters amplify the challenge. So, I sit in a circle, experiment with friends, practice independently, and offer this book to the world.

If you head down this path, I hope you enjoy the wild experience of whizzing past all the usual pleasantries to have a stranger tell you what you most need to hear—or be the person who provides that for another. But I hope it is not at the expense of everything you've learned here. I hope you continue to use your mediumship to connect to your body, excavate your mind, express your creativity, and build community.

Structuring a Reading

Like the structure of a message, a reading includes evidence, so the sitter can identify the contact, and information relevant to the sitter's current life. This is the content of the reading. In addition to content, which needs structure, there is also the context, which requires planning. The setting of the reading, how the medium prepares the sitter both before and at the beginning of the session, how long the reading lasts, how the medium ends the reading, and how they follow up (or not) all create the context. And while context matters for all forms of mediumship, it becomes the medium's sole responsibility, unlike the shared context of a circle. This section can be read from the perspective of a potential sitter or medium, thinking about how you might want to receive and give readings in the future.

Context

Getting the context right goes a surprisingly long way toward a good reading. The relative ease or challenge of scheduling, conditions of the surroundings, the medium's bedside manner, and timing all contribute to a solid and positive context that allows both the sitter and the medium to be comfortable to open up and hear what is said.

If you read for strangers, especially in person, there exist real safety precautions you'll need to consider. Although physical danger is rare in these situations, many people come to mediums in distress, so there is the potential for emotional and psychic harm, too. Consider how you will handle a situation where you feel physically, emotionally, or energetically endangered: What would you do if a client shows up unannounced? How could you leave a session if you need to? Whom can you call for help?

Scheduling

Mediumship readings are typically scheduled in advance. You could set up an open time, like at an event, for people to drop in. But most practically you will need a scheduling system for one-on-one readings. Having a calendar for potential clients to view your availability reduces the back and forth. Regardless, you must keep it current or risk people scheduling when you're unavailable. This can be a private link you only give to those who request it or an open link where anyone can request or book a specific time.

Scheduling may seem mundane to discuss at this point, but it sets the tone for the entire experience. Do both people show up? Do they arrive on time? Have they prepared? Do they know where to go and what to expect? How you book your readings could prepare everyone—or not. A few things to consider in addition to a live, online calendar: your code of conduct; a written explanation of your services (including what to expect and what to do before, during, and after); clearly articulated instructions for attending the session (including links for video chats, phone numbers plus who calls whom, addresses); written recording, refund, rescheduling, no-show, and lateness policies; automated reminders; and padding before and after sessions to give you a chance to recover and take care of yourself.

Location

Where will you hold your readings? If you are a sitter, where do you want to be? The phone offers privacy, but with it you have less to connect to for both parties. Video lets people remain in their own space, but you must consider how your environment affects you and the other person. Blurred or virtual backgrounds suffice for some types of meetings but can be disorienting and make things feel less "real." I do all my readings online and ensure I am in a clean room with little visual distraction for both our sakes.

If the reading is in a physical location, you may borrow or rent space or use some existing space you have. Set up comfortable seating for you and your clients, considering those who are disabled, have mobility or sensory issues, are people of size, come with a caretaker or loved one, and have other accessibility needs. You'll want seating not too close that your knees are touching but potentially close enough to take their hands (a common way to begin the connection).

You may be very comfortable in your own home, and so might another person, or they might not be. And how comfortable do you want them to be in your house? How do you get them to leave if they aren't ready? How much of your life do you want to share? Lily Dale has a generations-old tradition of reading rooms, tiny, enclosed front porches, or side entryways separated from the house. This elegant solution benefits from being in your own space with boundaries between living and working areas.

More than anything, the space must be quiet (visually and auditorily) and have no foot traffic. People cannot come in and out of your reading, disturbing you or the sitter in any way. Someone else overhearing it is inconsiderate and awkward.

Holding Space

Holding space is taking responsibility. With a reading, expect to hold the space for the sitter for the entire time. This contributes significantly to making readings so much work. Holding space means caring for the person from the moment they arrive until they walk back out the door—virtual or physical. This does not mean you can control what the other person does, but it does mean you moderate what you do to put their needs first. This is a radical act. A precarious act. One that isn't taken lightly. During the reading, you need to focus on them, making sure they are with you, that you listen to them, react to their feedback, and provide for their well-being.

Formal training in counseling, grief support, care work, conflict resolution, or other interpersonal skills will help prepare you to support your sitters better. This is on top of all our work with our contacts. The 2016 film *The Fundamentals of Caring* opens with Paul Rudd's character in a caretaker training course, learning ALOHA: Ask, Listen, Observe, Help, Ask again. I like this reminder of how involved understanding and tending to another's need is. It isn't as simple as one or two steps but a weaving of interactions and responses between people over time.

Sitters will cry. They may get upset, become unstable, push for more than you can give, or not be able to leave. These are real possibilities for which to prepare. Have a list of professionals you can refer clients to, such as other mediums, mental health practitioners, grief counselors, various medical professionals, and different types of energy workers. The NT2TD website and Resources section of this book will have a few to get you started. You'll need to find local support as well. This is also where your preparations during scheduling come into play. If you have clear rules for your readings that the client is already familiar with, it will be easier to say, "Our time is up, and I need you to leave now."

Timing

You may love giving readings so much that you will do them for hours and hours. I sometimes volunteer for Lily Dale events, giving ten-to-twenty-minute messages to individual sitters in the crowded and loud auditorium or fire hall. I usually feel downright loopy after a few hours. The tried-and-true Lily Dale offering is a thirty-minute reading. I've experimented with offering between ten minutes and an hour, and each time frame needs its own structure. Less than a half hour and you can't get in very deep; more than a half hour becomes tiring. Adding in regular psychic information or other types of healing work can fill up a longer time frame, but evidential mediumship for more than a half hour or so can get repetitive, with similar messages from different contacts. I usually offer forty minutes, which feels spacious, and I like to have at least twenty minutes between sessions.

Keeping time in a reading takes careful attention, and this is an important skill to learn early on. Make sure the reading lasts for the time you both agreed upon. I don't end a reading unless I've given some notice. That means I need to have seen a clock to calculate how much time remains and let the sitter know when to expect the session to end. Ensure you have a clock you can look at without distracting yourself or the sitter.

Also consider how often someone can come back for another reading. I limit my sitters to once per season—but I have worked with people monthly on occasion. I find readings more often than that become repetitive; this isn't the type of work that needs to be revisited frequently with a professional medium. Those who want more mediumship can learn, study, and participate in circles. When I have people booking frequent sessions, I ask what they're looking for and typically refer them to another practitioner.

Content

So you found someone who wants a reading. You found a time to meet. You sit down... but what do you do? Let's go through how to devise a structure for the content of your reading. You'll want to experiment and see what works for you, and like all the things we've learned until this point, this will take practice. In this case, you will need other people to practice with. In the Fellowships program, we had to submit documentation for each of our practice readings and healings using a survey we gave our sitters. This might be something to try if you enjoy receiving feedback. I still survey my sitters to ask about their experience of the elements of context and content. You can find a sample survey on the NT2TD website.

Welcome

You must find a way to start the reading. As with any meeting, introduce yourself and exchange names or pleasantries. Then I get right to it and ask if the person has had a reading before. This leads me to either the reading or the preamble. Another human sits in front of you who may be experiencing mediumship for the first time. Recall the first reading you received (go get one if you haven't yet!) and think about how it started. What made you feel comfortable or not? How did the medium shift from talking to the reading itself? While your mediumship will always be the focus of the sitter's attention, your bedside manner ensures they are ready and able to take in what you bring through.

The Preamble

If the person is new to mediumship or simply new to you, give a short overview of how you work. Sometimes I skip this with people I've worked with or change it based on what the sitter or I need to prepare. Explaining your process is a simple way to move from regular life into the reading. Of course, to explain how you work, you will have to know how you work. So, if it wasn't clear already, you must have done a lot of messages to arrive at that level of awareness. That's what circle is for—if you aren't ready, go back to the safe land where everyone knows what is happening and you don't need to explain. In most cases, all the welcoming and preamble take two or three minutes.

Here's an example from the beginning of the reading with a mother and her two adult daughters:

ME: What I'll do is take a moment when we're done getting set up, and I'll connect in. How I start is I'll go one person at a time, connect with your physical energy, more of a psychic connection, and bring in a little bit of information to ensure we're getting a good connection. And then I'll ask you if it's okay if I move into the spirit realm and see if any spirits want to join us. While bringing through information, I'll periodically ask if what I say makes sense. And all you need to do is say "yes," "no," or "I don't know." You don't have to give me any more information. I need to make sure we're on the right path and what I'm bringing through is useful.

The Shift

You will have to shift the interaction from regular communication to mediumship. I do this with a tiny, guided meditation that works as much for me as for the sitter. My goal is to get us out of everyday reality and into our bodies or an otherwise comfortable state conducive to discernment and connection. I want to give the sitter a clear understanding of their role—to stay in their internal experience and let my words wash over them.

Here's an example for someone who has had many readings (although it was their first with me):

ME: As you know, you can just sit there and relax and pay attention to your own inner thoughts and feelings, and any memories that come up or sensations that arise. Know that whatever happens internally for you is the guidance that you're meant to receive. No matter what the words I'm saying are, you have the ultimate answers in your internal world. I will take a minute of quiet, and then I will connect with you, if that's okay.

Connecting

Mediumship in front of and for someone who is not a medium is different than in a circle or class where you exchange from the same footing. In a reading, you essentially have a spectator. This is enough for many people to never bother with mediumship. There is potential for performance anxiety. You will need to be comfortable enough with your ability to connect that you can do it while a stranger is staring at you a foot away. Yes, you can close your eyes, but only part of the time. Yes, you can hold their hands, but only part of the time. Yes, you can scribble or do whatever you do to connect, but only part of the time. You must talk to them for most of the session as if everything is normal.

When I do a reading, I start by connecting psychically with the sitter and giving them a little information about themselves. This is how I evolved the Fellowships requirements for healing sessions into my mediumship practice. This step helps me learn about them and what is happening in their lives. I can check if the issue I see is what they hope to address and use that to guide the mediumship work. I also ask if they want to use tarot and will bring in the cards for those who do. But at some point I must stop that part of the reading (usually after five minutes) and shift to connecting to the spirit realm. Here's an example of this initial psychic connection from a sitter I had worked with once before.

ME: And as I connect in with you, I feel a deep wave of love and gratitude. I feel a deep feeling, a buzzing feeling as if there's been a lot of energy and activity going, especially toward healing, especially deep in the core of your body. Like, there's just been a lot going on to reregulate your systems. It's as if a lot of tangles needed to be kind of straightened out, smoothed out. And I just, I feel such a warm and loving presence as I connect in with you. And I feel how much your energy is expanding outward and how much energy you've needed to expend these past few months to heal and get the help and support you've needed. And I feel an upwelling of energy starting to emerge or starting to form that feels like it's going to work its way from the very core outward to all the way outside of your physical body. I feel like your energy is quite large and you have a lot you hold. Does that make sense to you?

SITTER: It's exactly what's been going on.

And here's how the connecting went for an experienced sitter I hadn't worked with before.

ME: I can feel you expanding in both the upward and downward directions, as if you're putting in roots and digging in, but also expanding upward and toward the sun. And I feel how much energy you're putting out right now to put yourself in the world in these ways and that it feels like there hasn't been a break for a while, it's been pretty steady. I get the feeling that you really move in a seasonal way, that whether it's aligned with the actual seasons or not, you go through long periods with intense energetic output, and then you get a little bit of a break, and then it's intense again. Does that feel right to you?

SITTER: Yes.

ME: All right. So I want to use that connection we have to move into the spirit realm. And is that okay with you?

SITTER: Yes.

Structuring the Reading

I have seen two main types of reading structure. Category-led readings are more common with sitters and practitioners used to psychic work. But they can still make an effective mediumship reading by focusing on key areas of the sitter's life.

Mediums more often work contact by contact. Each time we go into the spirit realm, we bring a contact and their message to the sitter and will do that either until the time is up or there aren't any more contacts left with messages.

Questions

Mediums vary in how much their sitters are expected to speak in a mediumship reading. The structure is very different between, say, therapy and mediumship. During the preamble, I usually tell my sitters that I will ask them questions periodically to check that I'm on the right track, and all I want them to respond with is "yes," "no," or "I don't know." At the end of the message, with any contact, I ask if they have a question. That's all the talking my sitters do. If I have a reading where the sitter has spoken much more than that, I often feel uneasy because I was trained that the medium provides information, not the sitter. And the more the sitter talks, the more information I have from the sitter, meaning the less time I have to get information from elsewhere. This can also signal that my sitter needs a practitioner focused on listening.

Closing and Aftercare

Along with issues of timing, readings need an emotional and energetic closing. I close the connection verbally and move the session back to regular life. Then we talk about how to reenter the day. The advice I give my sitters applies to me, too. We must be gentle with ourselves. Do something human, like walking, drinking water, or eating chocolate. And allow the experience to unfold.

When working alone, I sometimes think through the experience afterward. In general, with other people's messages and readings, I do not return to them, as that is too personal to do without the sitter. Many mediums develop the ability not to commit readings to memory as a healthy way to draw a boundary between other people's spiritual work and our own.

READING CHECKLIST

1. Find someone to give a thirty-minute reading to, considering these elements as you prepare:

   * **Who?** Choose someone with familiarity with this work who can let you read without interjecting or expecting something specific.

   * **Where?** Do you prefer online, by phone, or in person? In any case, where can you sit undisturbed for a half hour?

   * **When?** At what time of day can you find the time to prepare before the reading and decompress after? Do you feel more connected during certain parts of the day?

   * **Why?** Be prepared to explain that you are a student and want to practice. Ask for their understanding if the information you offer during the reading needs to be clarified or revised.

   * **How?** Prepare a short explanation of how you work to orient them to what will happen throughout the session.

   * **What?** Outline a structure you will use for this length of reading and allow for time at the end for the sitter to give you feedback on the context and the content of the reading.

2. Return to your list of support people from Chapter 3. Update it to prepare you for work with other people. Create your list of other providers to refer clients to in case they need support.

3. Go back to the Ethics and Boundaries sections in Chapter 3 and review Heidi Light's work. Update your list of boundaries and use it to develop your own code of conduct that you can share with your sitters.

Receiving Professional Care

Sometimes we need someone with more experience to help us find our way or who does things differently and can inspire us in a new direction. Mediumship is like dancing—you can do it as much or as little as you'd like. Even professional dancers watch other professional dancers. We don't all have the same taste in dance. And nobody became a professional dancer without watching and learning from many professionals along the way. If you are serious about developing your mediumship, I recommend watching demonstrations and visiting a variety of experienced mediums for one-on-one readings. Typically these will require payment, so it might not be accessible for everyone or all the time. But when you can, there is a lot to learn watching a pro, not only from a content perspective but to experience their approach to context.

If someone is in a place where they need care, including a mediumship reading, they are vulnerable. This is not typically the case when people look for a great dance show. Needing help is a fact of life—it happens to everyone and can't be avoided, but it can be treated with consideration and skill. Even after years as a provider, I sometimes want to book a reading in desperation. I have learned to take time to care for myself, ask for help from my social circle, and formulate straightforward questions before I book, which makes for much better results from readings.

If you read for strangers, know that people will come to you in crisis, grief, confusion, and deeply vulnerable places. Think of other kinds of care workers. Many take significant training and, typically, certification to provide therapy, counseling, coaching, or advice. When people come to professionals, they usually need some real help. Think of a customer service line. How often do you find yourself calling a company for help? When you do, what type of emotional state are you typically in? Now replace billing and technical issues with some of life's most significant challenges, like the death of a loved one or finding your purpose.

This is not a world to approach casually or carelessly. If we study, train, practice, and become a competent and fair medium, we can help people feel better in ways many see as magic. This leaves two more challenges for us to navigate: the power of helping people and having a skill most people lack. Having a stranger sit in front of me silently while I describe the person they loved the most is an unusual experience. They may have tears of joy at the recognition I offer of their loss, the reconnection, or the clarification. It is an unusual power to profoundly affect another person in a matter of moments. It is one thing for a doctor or artist to do this; it is another for someone professing a skill our society doesn't accept as genuine. Many believe that mediumship is magic. I want people to know it isn't magic. It is enough to have the power to affect people. We don't need magical powers as well—that is too much for anyone to manage.

The Constant Specter of Fraud

The association of deception with mediumship is not inevitable. I can imagine it's less of an issue in cultures with more exposure to the practice and in those offering more community and care for their mediums. This is not our lot. Fraud is an issue not only in mediumship but across the psychic services industry and many other fields associated with care. If money changes hands, there is the potential for someone to take advantage of another. Any time the vulnerable must pay for care, chances increase that the seeker will fall prey to an unscrupulous provider. Anytime the buyer does not understand a practitioner's service well, chances increase that subpar services will be rendered.

In Spiritualism, there have been two bombshell accounts of fraud and countless less shocking or well-publicized ones. Both come from high-profile Spiritualists whose relationships with the community had soured. In her fifties, one of the Fox sisters, credited with being the founders of modern Spiritualism as teenagers, gave interviews disclosing that all their work had been fraudulent, using the sounds of their toes cracking to make it appear they talked to the dead. This culminated in a letter to the *New York Herald* detailing the decades of deception. She later recanted the admission. The other is the account from M. Lamar Keene published in his book *The Psychic Mafia* (Prometheus Books, 1997). Keene shares not only how he faked readings and séances but exposed a ring of other Spiritualist mediums who collected personal information about sitters to use as evidence in messages.

These scandals remind us that mediumship can be faked. There are people out there who want to do that. By sharing how mediumship works, I aim to increase the number of ethical mediums providing services, pushing the fraudulent ones out of the market as better-educated customers come to the reading room with higher standards. Reading this book prepares you to evaluate mediums and their services. These skills are helpful:

* **Reducing urgency:** Strengthen your relationships with the dead, as well as with yourself and your community. This will provide you with more resources to confirm your reality, handle crises, envision the future, and uncover your purpose (a few of the most common reasons for readings).
* **Improving intuition:** Develop your ability to pick up on external and internal cues that something is off.
* **Self-trust:** Believe in your ability to know your assessment is correct and to act on it.

In my survey, I asked practitioners what they wished their clients knew about their work. Here's a summary of their responses:

1. This is a unique activity:
    * It's a special, intimate, and sometimes vulnerable process, rather than a performance or entertainment.
    * It requires significant effort, energy, and discipline from the practitioner.

- The process is fluid, creative, and involves many layers of insight and healing.
- Clients often receive what they need, not necessarily what they expect or want.
- The experience is distinct for each individual and session.
- Practitioners are facilitators, not all-knowing entities.

2. Working with psychic information isn't easy:
   - Practitioners don't curate or control the information; they relay what comes through.
   - Specific desired messages only sometimes come through as expected.
   - Messages can be subtle and may take time to understand or manifest.
   - Different types of energy (intuitive, psychic, mediumistic) are involved.

3. The client has an important role:
   - Clients have their own intuitive abilities and can often receive information themselves.
   - The process is collaborative, and clients' openness and participation enhance the experience.
   - Everyone has psychic capabilities, although they may manifest differently than expected.
   - Healing and mediumship are interconnected processes.
   - Personal spiritual practice evolves and grows over time.

4. There are limitations to this work:
   - Spirits are not all-knowing and may only sometimes communicate clearly.
   - The process has ethical guidelines and boundaries that practitioners follow.
   - It's not about ego or wealth for genuine practitioners.

Offering Readings

- * The work requires a profound depth of energy and can be emotionally taxing.
- * Practitioners often feel vulnerable and misunderstood in society.

5. The bottom line:
   - * The work involves multiple dimensions and energies coming together.
   - * The purpose is to empower clients to build their inner wisdom and spiritual connections.
   - * The process is part of the client's and practitioner's ongoing spiritual evolution.

---

1. What should a reading entail? Can you envision any improvements on the generally accepted format?

2. Do you want to make money by offering mediumship services? What type of clients do you want to have? What type of care will you need to provide them besides mediumship services?

3. How do you envision reciprocated mediumship in an ideal world? Are there other cultural or historical contexts for spiritual or energetic work that appeal to you?

4. What is your mediumship process now that you've had more experience? How do you need or want to adapt the process you've developed?

PREPARING FOR A READING

When I started giving readings, I had a ten-minute meditation I went through before every single one, even if I did them back to back. It was something like this:

I sit down, close my eyes, and notice my breath. I begin with deep cleansing breaths, filling up as much as possible and exhaling as much as possible. On an exhale, I let go of all the pieces of myself that are no longer needed. I see these pieces fall away, back into the earth. With a deep breath, I exhale and let go of all the pieces of others, from this realm or any other, that have attached to me or I have taken, knowingly or unknowingly, allowing them all to drift back to where they came from and where they belong. With a deep inhale, I call back to myself all the parts that have been lost, taken, or forgotten, bringing my true nature to fullness. With this, I breathe in, expanding and exploring the new space I've created, bringing strength for new parts of me to grow as the old parts fall away.

I take a moment in my mind to make space for new information. I feel into my heart to understand how I am showing up today. I notice the sensations of my body moving, as I need to ensure I am comfortable, supported, and safe. I allow my soul to be fully present with me as I engage in this practice.

I open my connection to the spirit realm, asking for the presence of my teachers, protectors, loved ones, and guides. I ask for only information for healing and empowerment for myself, my sitter, and all beings, and that those who wish to do harm are kept away from this place and this time, leaving me the safety to feel connected with myself, spirit, and my sitter.

CONCLUSION

On the sixth anniversary of my arrival in Lily Dale, the house was ready for me to throw a party. For the first time I invited my neighbors into my little cottage. I don't drink anymore, so I made a hot chocolate bar, and we crammed into my living room, dining room, and kitchen to celebrate New Year's 2024 (at 7:00 p.m.). Luncheons have resumed and this year there were two new people under forty years old at our annual meeting. Now, when I walk around the streets of Lily Dale with Coyo, I know every neighbor. A ten-minute stroll may take thirty because I stop and chat with a half dozen people. Yes, we complain about the weather and squabble over local politics. We also convey hellos from neighbors who have passed and swap insights into the meaning of life. I have finished my renovations and could rent out my house and move somewhere with shorter winters or a better (existent) dating scene. But I haven't. I can do my work anywhere, but nowhere else do I have so many living people I know and care for.

Now, when people ask if I'm a medium, I always say yes. I might not be the kind of medium that everyone expects, but I am making the practice my own.

The Future of Mediumship

There is an oft-cited prophecy in Modern American Spiritualism that was brought forward by Emma Hardinge Britten, a famous early medium and one of the original historians of the movement. She said that Spiritualism would have three phases: fifty years of joyful expansive growth, a period of misdirected sensationalism, and finally, contraction into religion. Spiritualism has seen all three stages of her strikingly accurate prediction. So where are we now?

The fourth phase of Spiritualism could be a return to the expansion found in the first. Many people practice mediumship in their own way or with groups that don't have the characteristics (particularly white Protestant adjacency) that aligned phase three Spiritualism with the dominant society. That alignment allowed mediumship, contained inside a legally and socially acceptable religion, to survive when the practice could be met with disdain and prosecution. Openness of approach and diversity of people were traded, consciously and unconsciously, for stability and survival. We have made it through the early scandals and McCarthyism, and civil rights have come a long way. While the work is far from complete, the wider culture is safe enough to open things back up for mediumship and the full breadth of mediums waiting to emerge. Perhaps this time around, mediumship will be able to forgo the rigid social expectations of the past.

I offer the terms *embodied mediumship* and *transphysical communication* for an expanded approach to the practice. They hint toward a world of connection and communication that begins within and goes beyond. I offer this book as a way for us to find our internal experience of love and mystery. With it, I hope we can unite to push past the sanctioning of mediumship within a religion toward the radical (and classically Modern American Spiritualist) idea that science, art, and community empower mediumship, too. These shifts are meant to welcome all those who are curious and anyone who employs their tools of care and connection to the beyond. Spiritualism of all types can hold its place in the center of it all, providing an enduring system grounded in history and established practice. Combine that with a wider movement fueling growth and experimentation, and we have a path to the collective advancement of all.

Conclusion

In this new era, we could do more than just talk to the dead. We have other frontiers presenting themselves now. The spirit realm calls to us—and so does the natural world, the farthest reaches of space, and the power of technology. Mediumship's foundations in imagination and relating bring us closer to ourselves, unite us across surface-level divides, and help us out of our speciesist, material-bound box. We need strong connections to ourselves and we need strong connections to each other.

Enjoy your time as a medium with all the connections you make, from your own body to all the life around you, in creativity and with supportive community. May they help you find yourself, and may they take you beyond.

NOTES

CHAPTER 1. MEDIUMSHIP IS FOR EVERYONE, JUST NOT ME

3 *Mediumship Is for Everyone*: A deferential nod to bell hooks and all her work. *Feminism Is for Everybody: Passionate Politics* (South End Press, 2000).

12 *In the spring of 2023*: Patricia Tevington and Manolo Corichi, "Many Americans Report Interacting with Dead Relatives in Dreams or Other Ways," Pew Research Center, August 23, 2023, https://www.pewresearch.org/short-reads/2023/08/23/many-americans-report-interacting-with-dead-relatives-in-dreams-or-other-ways/.

CHAPTER 2. CONCEPTUAL FRAMEWORKS

14 *Consciousness researcher and psychology professor*: Imants Barušs and Julia Mossbridge, *Transcendent Mind: Rethinking the Science of Consciousness* (American Psychological Association, 2017), 24.

15 *Only half of each of us are human cells*: Ron Sender, Shai Fuchs, and Ron Milo, "Revised Estimates for the Number of Human and Bacteria Cells in the Body," *PLoS Biology* 14, no. 8 (2016): e1002533, https://doi.org/10.1371/journal.pbio.1002533. There is additional work on this topic at https://www.humancellatlas.org/.

16 *Less than 10 percent of our DNA*: Nathan K. Schaefer, Beth Shapiro, and Richard E. Green, "An Ancestral Recombination Graph of Human, Neanderthal, and Denisovan Genomes," Science Advances 7, no. 29 (2021): eabc0776, https://doi.org/10.1126/sciadv.abc0776.

16 *One study showed that 81 percent*: https://windbridge.org/factsheets/WRC_accuracy.pdf.

16 *A meta-analysis of studies on mediums'*: Matthew Sarraf, Michael A. Woodley of Menie, and Patrizio Tressoldi, "Anomalous Information Reception by Mediums: A Meta-Analysis of the Scientific Evidence," EXPLORE 17, no. 5 (2021): 396–402, https://doi.org/10.1016/j.explore.2020.04.002.

18 *There are several passages in the Bible*: A tiny booklet printed in the 1920s by Rev. Merton W. Herbst includes fifty-one references in fourteen categories of the phenomena of spiritualism recorded in the Bible, such as spirit writing in Daniel v:5 and independent spirit voices in Ezekiel i:28.

28 *I cannot disprove this*: This is the first sentence of the Principle of Relativity from Einstein's "On the Foundations of a General Theory of Relativity," *Annalen der Physik* 55 (1918): 241–244. https://einsteinpapers.press.princeton.edu/vol7-trans/49. I learned of it in this paper: Marco Giovanelli, "Nothing but Coincidences: The Point-Coincidence and Einstein's Struggle with the Meaning of Coordinates in Physics," *European Journal for Philosophy of Science* 11, no. 45 (2021), https://doi.org/10.1007/s13194-020-00332-7.

36 *Although I no longer focus*: Learn more about my research and design work on my website https://nobox.us/.

Notes

CHAPTER 3. BEING A RESPONSIBLE MEDIUM

52 *As Deb Dana, LCSW, a clinician*: Deb Dana, *Polyvagal Exercises for Safety and Connection* (Norton, 2020). See page 132 for studies on co-regulation with nature. See page 118 for information on physical and imagined movement.

56 *When co-regulation is impaired*: Co-regulation, from a conversation between Stephen Porges, PhD, and Serge Prengel, LMHC. https://activepause.com/zug/transcripts/Porges-2016-09.pdf.

65 *Come up with something you*: This exercise is adapted from Sandra Ingerman's book *Soul Retrieval: Mending the Fragmented Self* (HarperOne, 2006).

PART II. THE REASON(S) FOR MEDIUMSHIP

72 *Martin Luther King, Jr.*: *The Autobiography of Martin Luther King, Jr.*, edited by Clayborne Carson (Warner Books, 1986).

73 *Our current systems are predicated*: My understanding of binaries, power, marginality, and mediumship were hugely influenced by *The Trickster and the Paranormal* by George P. Hansen (Xlibris Corp., 2001).

73 *To create a world that is*: Audre Lorde, "The Master's Tools Will Never Dismantle the Master's House," *Sister Outsider: Essays and Speeches*. (Crossing Press, 2007), 110–114.

CHAPTER 5. HEALING THROUGH CONNECTION

87 *I went from the*: Lily Dale has its own zip code, so we have hyperlocal data on our community you can see at https://data.census.gov/profile/ZCTA5_14752?g=860XX00US14752. For New York City data, see U.S. Census Bureau, "Population 65 Years and Over in the United States," *American Community Survey, ACS 1-Year Estimates Subject Tables, Table S0103*, 2022, accessed September 4, 2024, https://tinyurl.com/knj9bse4.

88 *The advisory shares that*: Office of the Surgeon General, "Our Epidemic of Loneliness and Isolation: The U.S. Surgeon General's Advisory on the Healing Effects of Social Connection and Community," US Department of Health and Human Services, 2023, https://www.hhs.gov/sites/default/files/surgeon-general-social-connection-advisory.pdf.

88 *More than lifestyle choices*: Ibid.

97 *In an interview, Dr. Stephen*: Co-regulation, from a conversation between Stephen Porges, PhD and Serge Prengel, LMHC. https://activepause.com/zug/transcripts/Porges-2016-09.pdf.

98 *When we lose*: There is some interesting information about building connection to the body in this article from Evlo: Shannon Ritchey, "Tools to Improve Muscle Activation & Results from Training," Evlo Fitness, May 17, 2023, https://evlofitness.com/education/improve-muscle-activation-results-from-training/.

111 *Barbara Kingsolver said in an interview*: Emily Bazelon and David Plotz, "How Charles Dickens Compelled an Author to Write the New *David Copperfield*," *Slate*, August 20, 2023, https://slate.com/culture/2023/08/book-charles-dickens-inspired-barbara-kingsolvers-demon-copperhead.html.

CHAPTER 6. IMAGINATION AS EXPLORATION

116 *The day we arrived in Lily Dale*: The National Oceanic and Atmospheric Administration (NOAA) has not-very-easy-to-use maps with historical climate data, and I was shocked to see it was even colder than I remembered! https://www.climate.gov/maps-data/dataset/past-weather-zip-code-data-table.

CHAPTER 7. MEDIUMSHIP FOR MONEY

134 *Although psychic services*: IBISWorld Industry Report OD4413 Psychic Service, April 2021.

136 *So, who has the money*: Lily Dale has a 19 percent employment rate versus 59 percent in New York State. For the surrounding area, Chautauqua County had a 4.3 percent unemployment rate in 2023 compared with a 3.4 percent national average. U.S. Bureau of Labor Statistics, "Unemployment Rate in Chautauqua County, NY," retrieved from FRED, Federal Reserve Bank of St. Louis, July 20, 2024, https://fred.stlouisfed.org/series/NYCHAU5URN.

136 *In addition to having*: US Census Data for ZIP Code Tabulation Area ZCTA5 14752, https://data.census.gov/profile/ZCTA5_14752?g=860XX00US14752.

137 *The IBISWorld report on psychic services*: IBISWorld Industry Report OD4413 Psychic Services in the US 2021.

CHAPTER 8. FORMING METHODS

145 *People have built temples*: S. W. Porges, "Vagal Pathways: Portals to Compassion," in E. M. Seppälä, E. Simon-Thomas, S. L. Brown, M. C. Worline, C. D. Cameron, and J. R. Doty (eds.), *The Oxford Handbook of Compassion Science* (Oxford University Press, 2017): 189–202, https://psycnet.apa.org/record/2017-43847-015.

156 *I learned the phrase*: Payton Busker, "Gentle Consistency: The Secret Sauce to Long-Term Results," Evlo Fitness, November 22, 2022, https://evlofitness.com/education/gentle-consistency-the-secret-sauce-to-long-term-results/.

RESOURCES

CHAPTER 1. MEDIUMSHIP IS FOR EVERYONE, JUST NOT ME

Podcast

My podcast, originally called *Unknown Unknown* and now *BEYOND with Tiffany Hopkins*, is available on Lily Dale Radio and wherever you get your podcasts.

Channeling Processes

How to Write Your First Book, Lesson One: The 7-Minute Writing System by DailyOM. This course is no longer available, but there are many others here: https://www.dailyom.com/courses/creativity/.

Language of the Soul: Applying Universal Principles for Self-empowerment: An Agartha Workbook by Meredith Lady Young (Stillpoint Publishing, 1987) is a classic guide on channeling.

The Other Side and Back: A Psychic's Guide to Our World and Beyond by Sylvia Brown and Lindsay Harrison (Penguin, 2000) is a popular guide for psychic development.

To Touch the Soul: How to Become a Medium by Judith Rochester (Watermark Inc., 2016) is a classic workbook for learning mediumship.

CHAPTER 2. CONCEPTUAL FRAMEWORKS

Books

Altered States of Consciousness: Experiences Out of Time and Self by Marc Wittmann (MIT Press, 2023) examines emerging research on the neural underpinnings of altered consciousness.

American Cosmic: UFOs, Religion, Technology by D. W. Pasulka (Oxford University Press, 2019) examines how people interpret unexplainable experiences.

The Death and Resurrection Show: From Shaman to Superstar by Rogan Taylor (Anthony Blond, 1985) examines the evolution of show biz from the healing work of shamans.

Death as an Altered State of Consciousness: A Scientific Approach by Imants Barušs (American Psychological Association, 2023) investigates scientific data of anomalous death-related phenomena.

Determined: A Science of Life Without Free Will by Robert M. Sapolsky (Penguin Press, 2023) examines the science and philosophy of decision-making to see how little of it is conscious or in the moment.

The Embodied Mind: Cognitive Science and Human Experience by Francisco J. Varela, Evan Thompson, and Eleanor Rosch (MIT Press, 1991) pioneered connections among phenomenology, mindfulness, and science.

The Evolution of Imagination by Stephen T. Asma (University of Chicago Press, 2017) explores improvisation and creativity through neuroscience, evolution, animal behavior, philosophy, and psychology.

The Flip: Epiphanies of Mind and the Future of Knowledge by Jeffrey J. Kripal (Bellevue Literary Press, 2019) uses famous rationalists' accounts of spiritual awakening and emerging understanding of consciousness to present a path forward for unifying the humanities and sciences.

Flow: The Psychology of Optimal Experience by Mihaly Csikszentmihalyi (Harper Perennial Modern Classics, 1990) explores what creates the state of consciousness called flow and its positive effects on life.

The Master and His Emissary: The Divided Brain and the Making of the Western World by Iain McGilchrist (Yale Press, 2009) gives an overview of how the hemispheres of the brain function based on neuroscience and its effect on culture.

The Trickster and the Paranormal by George P. Hansen (Xlibris Corp., 2001) uses the concept of a trickster to explain why psychic phenomena and UFOs are problematic for science.

Quantum Strangeness: Wrestling with Bell's Theorem and the Ultimate Nature of Reality by George Greenstein (MIT Press, 2019) is an approachable exploration of quantum mechanics.

Research

Bigelow Institute for Consciousness Studies: https://www.bigelowinstitute.org/

The Institute of Noetic Sciences studies the interconnected nature of reality: https://noetic.org/

Rupert Sheldrake studies telepathy in animals and people: https://www.sheldrake.org/

The Telepathy Tapes introduces us to telepathic savants: https://thetelepathytapes.com/

Windbridge Research Center studies dying, death, and what comes next: https://www.windbridge.org/

Resources

Conferences and Scholarly Gatherings

Archives of the Impossible at Rice University has annual conferences that can be attended online or in person: https://impossiblearchives.rice.edu/.

Chacruna's Institute for Psychedelic Plant Medicines has a variety of events: https://chacruna.net/.

Inquiry into the Anomalous holds conferences. Find past recordings on *Engaging the Phenomenon* on YouTube: https://www.youtube.com/@EngagingThePhenomenon/videos.

Morbid Anatomy holds international symposiums: https://www.morbidanatomy.org/.

The Parapsychological Association has an annual conference: https://www.parapsych.org/.

The Philosophical Research Society has online and in-person events: https://www.prs.org/.

Shannon Taggert's Science of Things Spiritual symposium is held in Lily Dale every summer: https://www.shannontaggart.com/symposium.

Organizations

The Clown School offers online and in-person study of clowning and the physical theater arts. I especially enjoyed Caroline Dream's Rebel Clown and Mike Funt's Satire classes: https://www.theclownschool.com/.

IDEO's design thinking helped bring human-centered design to the world: https://designthinking.ideo.com/.

Jax Weschler at Social Design Sydney has a trauma-informed design research course: https://socialdesignsydney.com/training-trauma-informed-design-research-practice-process-methods/.

Liberatory design was developed by the National Equity Project as an approach to addressing equity challenges and change efforts in complex systems: https://www.nationalequityproject.org/frameworks/liberatory-design.

Harvard Implicit Bias studies has an online test you can take: https://implicit.harvard.edu/implicit/takeatest.html.

CHAPTER 3. BEING A RESPONSIBLE MEDIUM

Books

Boundaries and Relationships: Knowing, Protecting and Enjoying the Self by Charles Whitfield (HCI, 1994) was my introduction to boundaries as a foundational part of healthy relationships.

Resources

Drawing Down the Spirits: The Traditions and Techniques of Spirit Possession by Kenaz Filan and Raven Kaldera (Destiny Books, 2009) offers a wide-ranging look at spirit possession in the modern world.

Ethics in Energy Medicine: Boundaries and Guidelines for Intuitive and Energetic Practices by Heidi Light (North Atlantic Books, 2018) is the seminal text for developing mediumship ethics that do no harm.

My Grandmother's Hands: Racialized Trauma and the Pathway to Mending Our Hearts and Bodies by Resmaa Menakem (Cultural Recovery Press, 2017) examines white-body supremacy in America from the perspective of trauma and body-centered psychology.

Holotropic Breathwork: A New Approach to Self-Exploration and Therapy by Stanislav Grof and Christina Grof (SUNY Press, 2023) introduces accelerated breathing techniques to create a non-ordinary state of consciousness for healing and transformation.

Polyvagal Exercises for Safety and Connection: 50 Client-Centered Practices by Deb Dana (Norton, 2020) offers practices to tune into the nervous system and reshape its responses.

Polyvagal Safety: Attachment, Communication, Self-Regulation by Stephen W. Porges (Norton, 2021) is a selection of published studies on the role of safety in our lives.

Psychic Self-Defense by Dion Fortune (Weiser, 1930) is a detailed manual for safeguarding against paranormal malevolence based on the author's experiences in 1920s America.

The Polyvagal Theory: Neurological Foundations of Emotions, Attachment, Communication, Self-Regulation by Stephen W. Porges (Norton, 2011) is a compilation of Porges's decades of research.

The Power of Breathwork: Simple Practices to Promote Wellbeing by Jennifer Patterson (Fair Winds Press, 2020) is a guide to incorporating meditative breathing into daily life with twenty-five simple exercises.

Total I Ching by Stephen L. Karcher (Piatkus, 2009) is my favorite translation of the ancient Chinese divination text.

Waking the Tiger: Healing Trauma by Peter A. Levine (North Atlantic Books, 1997) is one of the seminal texts that illuminated how trauma is understood and treated.

What It Takes to Heal: How Transforming Ourselves Can Change the World by Prentis Hemphill (Random House, 2024) explains why personal healing is foundational to social change and how embodiment provides tools for both.

Resources

Mental Health Support Organizations

The Emergent Phenomenology Research Consortium explains the barriers to receiving care from medical professionals for those who experience anomalous phenomena: https://theeprc.org/.

Crisis lines, or lifelines, may route callers to police or other emergency support to connect them to resources as soon as possible. Text 988 or use the chat feature on http://988lifeline.org/. You can also contact the Crisis Text Line by texting HOME to 741741 at any time.

Warmlines provide a trained volunteer to talk to. There's a directory for warmlines across the United States and for many different languages at https://www.warmline.org/#directory.

Inclusive Therapists can help you find a mental health provider and has a list of community-led warmlines at https://www.inclusivetherapists.com/crisis.

There is not a warmline specifically for people who have experienced anomalous events. If you need to speak with someone who understands mediumship, you can reach out to a minister at your nearest Spiritualist church for help.

Breathwork Providers

Debbie Attias, Fun Heals Everything: https://www.funhealseverything.com/

Jennifer Patterson, Corpus Ritual: https://corpusritual.com/

Patricia Price: https://www.patriciaprice.com/

Luke Simon: https://lukesimonmystic.com/

Erin Telford: https://www.erintelford.com/

Anabel Zenith: https://www.anabelzenith.com/

CHAPTER 4. NOT QUITE BORN AGAIN

Books

A Luminous Brotherhood: Afro-Creole Spiritualism in Nineteenth-Century New Orleans by Emily Suzanne Clark (UNC Press, 2016) is the history of a group of Black men practicing Spiritualism in New Orleans beginning in the 1860s.

Black Spiritual Movement by Hans A. Baer (University of Tennessee Press, 1984) includes Spiritualism in an investigation of the Black Spiritual movement in the United States.

Resources

Body and Soul: A Sympathetic History of American Spiritualism by Robert S. Cox (University of Virginia Press, 2003) posits that Spiritualism was the transformation of sympathy into social practice.

Chronicles of Lily Dale by Ron Nagy with Joyce LaJudice (2017) gives a year-by-year overview of the development of Lily Dale.

Dancing in the Streets: A History of Collective Joy by Barbara Ehrenreich (Metropolitan Books, 2006) explores humanity's oldest traditions of collective celebration and their repression.

Ghostly Communion: Cross-Cultural Spiritualism in Nineteenth-Century American Literature by John J. Kucich (Dartmouth College Press, 2004) examines how Spiritualism mediated cross-cultural conflict and negotiation in the United States.

Ghosts of Futures Past: Spiritualism and the Cultural Politics of Nineteenth-Century America by Molly McGarry (University of California Press, 2008) looks at how the once-marginalized practice of talking to the dead came to the center of American cultural history.

The History of Spiritualism by Arthur Conan Doyle (1926) is an early history of Modern American and British Spiritualism.

Lily Dale: The True Story of the Town That Talks to the Dead by Christine Wicker (HarperCollins, 2003) explores Lily Dale from the stories of three female residents.

Modern American Spiritualism by Emma Hardinge Britten (1870) covers the first twenty years of the movement.

Notorious Victoria by Mary Gabriel (Algonquin Books, 1998) is a biography of the famous radical Victoria Woodhull, showing she was taken seriously by her contemporaries although she was largely written out of history.

Other Powers: The Age of Suffrage, Spiritualism, and the Scandalous Victoria Woodhull by Barbara Goldsmith (Random House, 1988) gives the story of Victoria Woodhull in the context of Reconstruction and the splintering of progressives over supporting Black men or white women for the right to vote.

The Psychic Mafia by M. Lamar Keene (Prometheus Books, 1997) is a tell-all account of a self-proclaimed fake Spiritualist medium.

Radical Friend: Amy Kirby Post and Her Activist Worlds by Nancy A. Hewitt (University of North Carolina Press, 2018) reacquaints us with a pillar of radical activism in nineteenth-century America.

Resources

Radical Spirits: Spiritualism and Women's Rights in Nineteenth-Century America by Ann Braude (Beacon Press, 1989) examines how Spiritualism empowered a generation of women in the United States.

Raising the Dead: Readings of Death and (Black) Subjectivity by Sharon Patricia Holland, (Duke University Press, 2000) includes Spiritualism in this literary investigation of death, race, sexuality, and gender in twentieth-century American culture.

The Reluctant Spiritualist: The Life of Maggie Fox by Nancy Rubin Stuart (Harcourt Books, 2005) gives the story of one of the women at the heart of the religious, social, and spiritual upheavals of her time.

Speaking to the Dead in Early America by Erik R. Seeman (University of Pennsylvania Press, 2019) gives a 300-year history of Protestant relationships with the dead.

Podcast

Unobstructed's second season gives a compelling and deep overview of Modern American Spiritualist history: https://www.grimandmild.com/unobscured.

CHAPTER 5. HEALING THROUGH CONNECTION

Books

All About Love: New Visions by bell hooks (William Morrow Paperbacks, 1999) is the book everyone needs for learning about love, along with the other two books in the series, *Salvation* and *Communion*.

Ancestral Medicine: Rituals for Personal and Family Healing by Daniel Foor, PhD (Bear & Company, 2017) is a practical guide for navigating relationships with the spirits of ancestors.

An Immense World: How Animal Senses Reveal the Hidden Realms Around Us by Ed Yong (Random House, 2022) and his earlier book *I Contain Multitudes: The Microbes within Us and a Grander View of Life* (Ecco, 2016) both look at other ways to see the world.

The Body Is Not an Apology: The Power of Radical Self-Love by Sonya Renee Taylor (Berrett-Koehler Publishers, 2018) is an invitation to transform the world starting with how we feel about ourselves.

Bowling Alone: The Collapse and Revival of American Community by Robert D. Putnam (Simon & Schuster, 2000) is an overview of shifting social behaviors in the United States through the twentieth century.

Breath: The New Science of a Lost Art by James Nestor (Riverhead Books, 2020) teaches us about that thing we do 25,000 times a day.

Resources

Entangled Life: How Fungi Make Our Worlds, Change Our Minds & Shape Our Futures by Merlin Sheldrake (Random House, 2020) changes our perspective by showing us the world from a fungal point of view.

Feeding Your Demons: Ancient Wisdom for Resolving Inner Conflict by Tsultrim Allione (Little Brown and Company, 2008) adapts for the present time an ancient method of coping with inner demons developed by Tibet's most renowned female Buddhist leader, Machig Labdrön.

Leaving My Father's House: A Journey to Conscious Femininity by Marion Woodman (Shambala Publications, 1992) includes the personal journeys of three women toward psychic wholeness through Jungian analysis.

Nature and the Human Soul: Cultivating Wholeness and Community in a Fragmented World by Bill Plotkin (New World Library, 2008) addresses the pervasive longing for meaning and fulfillment by shifting modern human development from ego-centric to eco-centric.

On Looking: A Walker's Guide to the Art of Observation by Alexandra Horowitz (Scribner, 2013) and her earlier book *Inside of a Dog: What Dogs See, Smell and Know* (Scribner, 2010) offer alternative ways of seeing the world as shared by a cognitive scientist.

On Repentance and Repair: Making Amends in an Unapologetic World by Danya Ruttenberg (Beacon Press, 2022) offers five steps toward healing both personal transgressions and our culture's most painful unresolved issues.

Personal Mythology: Using Rituals, Dreams, and Imagination to Discover Your Inner Story by David Feinstein and Stanley Krippner (Energy Psychology Press, 2008) is a twelve-week program for understanding and transforming personal and cultural patterns.

Rest Is Resistance: A Manifesto by Tricia Hersey (Little, Brown Spark, 2022) illuminates the liberatory power of rest, daydreaming, and naps.

Ritual: Power, Healing and Community by Malidoma Patrice Somé (Compass, 1997) brings together practices of West African Dagara and modern Western culture.

A Wild and Sacred Call: Nature-Psyche-Spirit by Will W. Adams (SUNY Press, 2023) explores the dynamic between consciousness, culture, and relationship to help address the ecological crisis.

The Wisdom of Wildness: Healing the Trauma of Domestication by Ren Hurst (Findhorn Press, 2022) examines the nature of domestication and humanity's relationships with other animals.

CHAPTER 6. IMAGINATION AS EXPLORATION

Books

Freedom Dreams: The Black Radical Imagination by Robin D. G. Kelley (Beacon Press, 2003) shares visions of activists and the power of imagination to transform society.

We Do This Til We Free Us: Abolitionist Organizing and Transforming Justice by Mariame Kaba (Haymarket Books, 2021) shows us how ordinary people have the power to collectively free ourselves.

Stay Woke: A Meditation Guide for the Rest of Us by Justin Michael Williams (Sounds True, 2020) is a modern approach to mindfulness that acknowledges and addresses the struggles that keep us from meditating.

Don't Just Sit There: 44 Insights to Get Your Meditation Practice Off the Cushion and Into the Real World by Biet Simkin (Simon & Schuster, 2018) is an easy-to-read advice book for developing a meditation practice.

Providers

Insight Timer has free mindfulness tools for sleep, anxiety, and stress: https://insighttimer.com/.

Open's classes combine traditions and technologies to explore greater collective presence and awareness: https://o-p-e-n.com/.

The Rubin Museum's *Mindfulness Meditation* podcast has many hours of lovely meditations: https://rubinmuseum.org/page/mindfulness-meditation-podcast/.

Articles

National Equity Project teaches freedom dreaming: https://www.nationalequityproject.org/blog/freedom-dreaming.

Psyche magazine teaches mental time travel and many other topics: https://psyche.co/guides/feeling-overwhelmed-in-the-present-try-mental-time-travel.

CHAPTER 7. MEDIUMSHIP FOR MONEY

People

Find Grace Kredell online: https://www.gracekredell.com/ and Kredell, Grace, "Working Witches: Fortune Tellers, Clairvoyants, and Astrologers in the Golden Age of Spiritualism," *Women's History Theses* 64 (2022), https://digitalcommons.slc.edu/womenshistory_etd/64.

Find Dr. Michelle Barr online: https://michellebarr.com/ and see her book: *From Calling to Cash: Turn Your Life's Calling into a Profitable Business You Love* (2019).

Find Celeste Elliott online: https://www.celesteelliott.com/.

Books

Caliban and the Witch: Women, The Body and Primitive Accumulation by Silvia Federici (Autonomedia, 2004) is the history of the body in the transition to capitalism.

Care Work: Dreaming Disability Justice by Leah Lakshmi Piepzna-Samarasinha (Arsenal Pulp Press, 2018) is a great resource for understanding the challenges of disabled and chronically ill people and how to build liberation and accessibility in your community.

Caste: The Origins of Our Discontents by Isabel Wilkerson (Random House, 2020) explores how America has been shaped by a rigid hierarchy of human rankings, linking it to caste systems worldwide.

Universal Design for Learning (UDL) for Inclusivity, Diversity, Equity, and Accessibility (IDEA) by Darla Benton Kearney gives an introduction to positionality and intersectionality: https://ecampusontario.pressbooks.pub/universaldesign/chapter/positionality-intersectionality/.

CHAPTER 9. MEDIUMSHIP FOR CREATIVITY

Books

The Artist's Way: A Spiritual Path to Higher Creativity by Julia Cameron (Tarcher Perigee, 1992) is a twelve-week program that uncovers the link between the spiritual and creative self.

Bird By Bird: Some Instructions on Writing and Life by Anne Lamott, (Knopf Doubleday, 1995) was the first book I read on writing and it has always stuck with me.

The Book on Mediums: Guide for Mediums and Invocators by Allan Kardec (Weiser, 1874) is a cornerstone of Spiritism, a religion related to Spiritualism that is especially popular in France and Brazil.

The Creative Act: A Way of Being by Rick Ruben (Penguin Publishing Group, 2023) illuminates the artist's role as one in relationship to the world.

The Creative Habit: Learn It and Use It for Life by Twyla Tharp (Simon & Schuster, 2006) offers inspiration and practical advice for building a creative practice.

D.I.Y. Magic: A Strange & Whimsical Guide to Creativity by Anthony Alvarado (Perigee, 2012) offers techniques for reaching deeper levels of creative thought and accessing the subconscious.

Fingerpainting on the Moon: Writing and Creativity as a Path to Freedom by Peter Levitt (Harmony Books, 2003) shows how spirituality and creativity work together.

The Other Side: A Journey into Women, Art, and the Spirit World by Jennifer Higgie (Weidenfeld & Nicolson, 2023) explores the lives and works of women who communicate with other dimensions.

Writing Down the Bones: Freeing the Writer Within by Natalie Goldberg (Shambala Publications, 1986) combines Zen meditation and writing to help writers develop their practice.

Classes

Anne-Marie Bond is based in the United Kingdom and teaches spirit art classes online: https://www.theportraitofspirit.com/mediumship-workshops/.

Arthur Findlay College has spirit and trance art courses: https://www.arthurfindlaycollege.org/subjects/art/.

Lily Dale Assembly has classes related to art and mediumship each season, including my own: https://www.lilydaleassembly.org/.

Morbid Anatomy often hosts creativity-related classes, including my mediumship for creativity series: https://www.morbidanatomy.org/.

Richard Stuttle teaches spirit art and other healing and creativity-focused workshops: https://www.richardstuttle.com/healing/.

Residencies

Normalize Talking to the Dead has a residency program where people can stay in my house and work on their connection skills. Learn more at www.normalizetalkingtothedead.com/residency.

Sacred Grounds, a coffee shop in Lily Dale, hosts an artist residency every summer. Learn more on their website: https://sacredgroundscoffeehouseld.com/.

The Whole Utopianotes Catalog includes residencies as part of resource-gathering and sharing for artists, writers, entrepreneurs, and other fellow travelers: https://adrianshirk.substack.com/.

Words of Mouth newsletter often has interesting opportunities in the arts: https://www.wordsofmouth.org/.

CHAPTER 10. DEVELOPMENT CIRCLES

Books

Rules to Be Observed when Forming Spiritual Circles by Emma Hardinge and Others (Colby and Rich, 1887) is a classic pamphlet on development circles you can get for free online: https://www.ehbritten.org/texts/primary/ehb_rules_to_be_observed_1887.pdf

Your Universal Spiritual Circle: A Step-By-Step Guide by Patricia Price (2018) is a short, practical approach to forming circles.

Resources

Spiritualist Churches and Schools

Arthur Findlay College teaches Spiritualist philosophy and religious practice, spiritual and psychic unfolding, and kindred disciplines: https://www.arthurfindlaycollege.org/.

City of Light Spiritualist Church has pet-friendly services in Lily Dale that are also streamed online: https://www.cityoflightspiritualistchurch.com/.

Church of the Living Spirit has services and events in Lily Dale and online: https://www.churchofthelivingspirit.org/.

Fellowships of the Spirit teaches meditation, intuitive development, mediumship, and spiritual healing: https://www.fellowshipsspirit.org/.

Lily Dale Assembly's summer program teaches various spiritual and wellness topics focusing on Spiritualism: https://www.lilydaleassembly.org/.

Lily Dale Spiritualist Church has services on the Lily Dale grounds: https://www.lilydalespiritualistchurchnsac.com/.

Morris Pratt teaches the religion, science, and philosophy of Modern American Spiritualism: https://morrispratt.org/.

The National Association of Spiritualist Churches has a directory of member Spiritualist churches: https://nsac.org/.

Spiritualist Church of New York City meets in Manhattan and online: https://www.spiritualistchurchnyc.com/.

Spiritualists' National Union International offers members affordable, in-depth Spiritualist education: https://snui.org.uk/.

Non-Spiritualist Communities

Academy of Oracle Arts is a school of sacred sciences, mystical arts, and mystery studies: https://www.academyoforaclearts.com/.

The Design Justice Network wields collective power and experiences to create safer, more just, more accessible, and more sustainable worlds: https://designjustice.org/events.

The Dream Hive is a schoolhouse for the soul, a space for spirit and community to cultivate bravery, courage, grace, and belonging: https://dreamhivenyc.com/.

Golden Dome is a community dedicated to mysticism and the arts: https://www.golden-dome.org/.

Resources

Imperialists Anonymous is an international fellowship of people in recovery from imperialism: https://imperialistsanonymous.org/.

Morbid Anatomy has online offerings as well as community collaborations related to death, life, and the in between: https://www.morbidanatomy.org/.

Normalize Talking to the Dead talks to the living about talking to the dead: http://normalizetalkingtothedead.com.

Showing Up for Racial Justice (SURJ) organizes white people to fight racism and envisions a just, vibrant future for all: https://surj.org/.

YES! connects, inspires, and collaborates with change-makers to build thriving, just, and regenerative ways of life for all: https://yesworld.org/.

CHAPTER 11. OFFERING READINGS

Books

Magickal Medium: Partnering with the Ancestors for Healing and Spiritual Development by Danielle Dionne (Llewellyn Books, 2022) combines Spiritualism, magick, and death positivity.

Medium Mentor: 10 Powerful Techniques to Awaken Divine Guidance for Yourself and Others by MaryAnn DiMarco (New World Library, 2022) is an approachable resource for developing mediums.

Modern Mediumship: A Complete (Woo-Woo-Free) Course to Become a Successful Psychic Medium by Johan Poulsen (2022) is a straightforward approach to client mediumship.

My Spirit Workbook by Celeste Elliot (2024) is a guided notebook for developing mediums.

Podcast

Ghost of a Podcast by Jessica Lanyadoo, an astrologer, psychic medium, and animal communicator, includes mediumship readings in some episodes: https://www.lovelanyadoo.com/ghost-of-a-podcast.

Lily Dale Radio airs programs by Lily Dale mediums and residents, including my show: https://www.youtube.com/@lilydaleassemblyinc.3638/streams.

INDEX

A
abolition, 80–81
accountability, 140
adaptation, 33
advice-giving, 44–45, 189
af Klint, Hilma, 164
affective charge, 34
alignment practice, 149
altars, ancestor, 114–115
altered states of consciousness, 46–49
American-style mediumship, 179, 180
analysis paralysis, 170
ancestor veneration, 18
ancestry, learning one's, 104–105
animal communication, 16. See also pets
apologies, conducting formal, 107
artistic composition. See creativity
artists, female, 164–165
asking, 148–149
Asma, Stephen T., 33
attention, 120–121, 130–132. See also imagination; presence
attentional travel, 125–127
attentional travel, practice of, 125–127
automatic work, 165, 171, 174
avoidance behaviors, 42
awareness
  energetic, 95
  heightened, 120

B
Bangs, May and Lizzie, 167
Barr, Michelle, 134, 139

Baruss, Imants, 14
biases, 29–32, 90
binaries, convenience of, 73
birthday party séances, 198–199
Black Americans, 85
Black Spiritual Movement, 85
body, the
  as an antenna, 96
  being present with, 95, 102–103
  connecting with, 102–103
  connection to, 102–103
  guided meditation, 91–92
  listening to, 53
  noticing the, 91–92
  reconnecting with, 54–56
  sensations in, 100–101
body posture, 96
body scan meditation, 103
boggle threshold, 14
Bond, Ann-Marie, 165–166
boundaries, 65–68, 141, 155, 171
brain, the, 28–31
breathwork, 57–59, 96
British-style mediumship, 179, 180
Britten, Emma Hardinge, 219–220
Busker, Payton, 156–157

C
Carlson, Charvonne, 78–79
Cassadaga Lake Free Association, 76–77
Cassadaga Lake, history of, 75–77
centering, 95
channeling, 7
clairalience, 26
clairaudience, 26

claircognizance, 25, 26, 63
clairempathy, 26
clairgustance, 26
clairsalience, 26
clairsentience, 26
clairtangency, 26
clairvoyance, 26
classical spiritualist model, 24
clichés, reliable, 34
closing a connection, 154–155
clowning, 35
cocreation, 93–94
confidentiality and privacy, 43–44
connection
  ancestry and, 104–105
  to the body, 102–103
  boundaries and, 171
  bringing pain, 94
  built on love, 93
  choosing a contact, 170–171
  closing, 154–155, 163
  cocreation, 93–94
  with the dead, 104
  developing, 156–157
  focus on, 72–73
  formal apologies process, 107
  forming, 148
  with guides and nonhuman contacts, 180–181
  influencing health, 88
  interfacing with physical and other realms, 114
  invitation to, 149
  with living lineage, 105
  permission for, 149
  with pets, 108
  with places, 109–111
  practicing, 144
  practicing with others, 160

Index

preparing for, 95–96
senses in, use of, 96–97
social, 90
spectrum of, 151–154
steps for, 162
with things, 112–113
turning on/off, habit of, 156–157
writing and, 172
consciousness, altered states of, 46–49
contact, defined, 21
contact points, 69–71
co-regulation, 56
creativity, 19
  act of, 160–161
  analysis paralysis, 170
  automatic vs independent work, 171
  automatic work, 165, 171, 174
  choosing a purpose, 167
  decision-making and, 174
  female artists, 164–165
  introduction to, 160–161
  mechanics of, 162–163
  meditation for, 168–169
  mediumship as helpful in, 163
  mediumship compared to, 161–162
  mediumship with, 172–173
  motivations for, 170
  philosophy of, 161–162
  precipitated paintings, 166–167
  ritualizing, 172–173
  skills required for, 162
  starting a project, 174
  types of, 164–167
  visionary, 174–175
creativity circle, 175
cultural appropriation, 83

D
Dana, Deb, 52, 57
data/data processing
  biases, 29–32
  defense mechanisms, 30–31
  defined, 21
  example of, 26–28
  externalizing, 150
  materialist approaches to, 22
  nonverbal, 108
  output, 32
  overview, 20–21
  raw, 21
  sources of, 21–22
  spiritualist approaches to, 24
  transphysical sources for, 23, 24, 26–28
  transverbal, 108
  trust-worthy, 62–63
dead projects, séances for, 199
decision-making. *See* discernment
defense mechanisms, 30–31
deity possessions, 69
development circles, 44. *See also* mediumship training
  behavior and boundary protocols, 193
  building rapport and trust, 197
  closed vs open, 191
  discretion outside of, 193
  example of, 176–177
  focus during, 192
  frequency of gatherings, 191
  leadership in, 191
  locations for, 192
  management of, 191
  membership in, 191
  one-on-one readings, 193
  opening and closing of, 194–195
  speaking time balance, 192
  starting, 190–193
  structure of, 192–193
  video conferencing and, 192
discernment, 60–64, 150, 174
discipline, self-imposed, 33
divination
  boundary setting, 65–68
  contact points, 69–71
  discernment and, 61–62
  overview, 63
  tethering practices, 71
dysregulation, state of, 51, 52

E
Ebenstein, Joanna, 125
Elliott, Celeste, 134
embodied mediumship, 24, 25, 95–96, 108, 220
embodiment, 94–96, 121
Emergent Phenomenology Research Consortium, 48
emotional regulation, 121
emotions, engaging with, 103
empathy, 94
energetic hygiene, 155
ethics, 40, 43–46
exclusion, 90
exercise, 57
expression, 150–151
external factors, protection from, 144–145
extrasensory perception (ESP), 15, 16

F
faith, in becoming a medium, 12
fees, 45
Fellowships of the Spirit, 6–7, 142–143, 200
female artists, 164–165
feminism, 82
Ferguson, Christine, 81
filters, 154
focus
  attentional travel and, 126
  breathing (*See* breathwork)
  connecting with the body, 102–103
  in development circles, 192
  finding, 65
  presence and, 121
  quieting, 144, 146–147
  shifting, 145

Index

foundational state, 120
Fox, George, 80
Fox sisters, 80, 214
fraudulent mediums, 214–217
freedom, 33
functional promiscuity, 34

G
gender equality, 82
ghostism, 41
Gill, Madge, 165
grief, 107
grounding, 95, 121

H
habit formation, 155–157
hands-on healing, 100, 102–103
Haudenosaunee Confederacy, 76
healing energy, when talking to the dead, 8
healing practices, 96
heart lineages, 106
Hemphill, Prentis, 65
Hicksites, 80
high-stakes conditions improvisation, 34
hot readings, 15
Houghton, Georgiana, 165
human-centered design, 36
humor, 35
hypnagogic state, 47

I
imagination
  developing the mind's eye, 131–132
  energetic resolutions, 130–131
  making it up vs, 117–119
  mapping out the upcoming year, 132
  modalities to, 117–118
  returning to ordinary state, 130–132
  revisiting the past, 132
  as safe way to transordinary reality, 117
  time and place exploration, 125–126
  vantage points, 131
imaginative faculties, 33
improvisation, 32–35
independent work, 171
indirect inspiration, 174
informed consent and permission, 43
insomnia, 123
inspiration, 174. *See also* creativity
interdependence, 140
interfaces, 114–115
intergenerational trauma, 52
intermediary states, 19
internal quiet, 145
interoception, 97, 100
interview/interviewing, 36–38, 149
intuition, 33, 42
invitation, as step in asking, 149

J
Jung, Carl, 108

K
Keene, M. Lamar, 215
King, Martin Luther, Jr., 72
Kingsolver, Barbara, 111
known dead, 104
Kredell, Grace, 134

L
Lanyadoo, Jessica, 199
laying on of hands. *See* hands-on healing
letting go, 120, 144, 145, 148
Light, Heidi, 43
Lily Dale, New York, 3–4, 75, 135–136. *See also* Cassada Lake
lineage, 105–107
listening, 96
living people
  connecting to, 105, 119
  distinction between nonliving and, 1–2
loneliness, 87–88
Lorde, Audre, 73

M
materialism, 14–17, 22
McGilchrist, Iain, 28–29
medication conditions/treatments, 48–49
meditations, guided
  for a creative project, 168–169
  feeling how mind and body produces data, 152–153
  moving attention into different places and times, 128–129
  noticing the body, 91–92
  opening and closing a development circle, 194–195
  preparing for a reading, 218
  to support quieting, 146–147
medium practitioners
  on becoming a, 12
  bedside manner of, 207
  bias and societal pressures of, 138–139
  defined, 2
  demographics, 136–137
  evaluating, 215–217
  fraudulent, 214–217
  functioning as (*See* data/data processing)
  hiring, ix
  professional (*See* professional mediumship)
  stigmatization of, 138
  types of writing done by, 163
  what clients should know about, 215–217
mediumship. *See also*

Index

responsible mediumship
as act of relating within internal experience, 6
American-style, 179, 180
as beneficial to everyone, 8
British-style, 179, 180
as a business (*See* professional mediumship)
client's role, 216
collective, 82
conceptual models of, 24-25
cultivating relationships, 196-197
defined, 1-2
economics of, 135-137
embodied, 24
experimental research on, 16
faith-based understanding of, 17-19
future of, 219-221
genetic inheritance of, 81-82
as intangible element of life, 12-13
integrating into life, ix
introduction to, viii-x
limitations to, 216-217
materialist approaches to, 14-17
method for (*See* mediumship development)
for money (*See* professional mediumship)
physical vs mental, 95, 163
readings (*See* readings)
as relational, 34
scandals, 214-217
sharing with someone else about, 196-197
spiritualist approaches to, 14, 17-19
training (*See* mediumship training)
trance, 22
as unique activity, 215
uses of, ix
mediumship development. *See also* connection
asking, 148, 149, 173
closing, 154-155, 173
connecting, 172
with creativity, 172-173
evaluating and developing, 158-159
expanding, 198-199
habit formation, 155-157
identification of contacts, 150
one-time, 198
overview, 142-143
quieting, 144, 172
receiving messages, 150, 173
translating messages, 150-151, 173
mediumship training
advice-giving and, 189
building rapport with sitters, 189
choosing a sitter, 180
choosing a spirit, 180
development circles and (*See* development circles)
getting stuck, 189-190
identifying a spirit, 181-184
message work, 178-180
off-limit items, 189
permission to give a message, 181
practicing with fellow mediums, 177-178
providing evidence to the sitter, 184-186
pushing past fear of sounding wrong, 177
real-time feedback, 177-178
receiving/conveying messages, 186-187
showing and telling messages, 187-189
mental clarity, 120
mental mediumship, 95, 163.
See also mediumship
Millar, Marza, 6, 41
mindfulness
presence and, 120-122
as an unlearning, 121-122
Modern American Spiritualism
abolition and, 80-81
author's research into, 78-79
Black Americans and, 85
closed-minded activities of, 85
cultural appropriation in, 83
early movement, 77-78
early Spiritualist tradition woven into, 79
foundation in science and philosophy, 79
foundational principle of, 4
future of, 219-221
history of, 79-85
individual responsibility, foundation of, 81-82
Quakerism and, 81
regressive movements, 85
as a religion, 17-18
as a religious add-on, 79-80
respectability politics in, 84
as spiritual but not religious, 83
as women-led movement, 82
modern life, defining traits of, 89-90
Morbid Anatomy, 78
motivations, 170
mourning circles, 198
movement, 56-57, 96

N

Nagy, Ron, 78
named dead, 104
National Colored Spiritualist Association of Churches, 85
National Spiritualist Association, 84, 85

Index

National Spiritualist Association of Churches (NSAC), 84
natural world, connection to, 103, 110, 111
neuroception, 14, 50
neurological states, 51–52
New Age beliefs, 18
nonliving persons. *See also* spirit realm/spirits
  connecting with, 1
  distinction between living and, 1–2
  healing energy experienced when talking to, 8
  humans' relationship with, 78
non-ordinary states, 46–49
nonverbal data, 108

O

objectivity, 44–45
observation, state of, 145
one-on-one readings. *See* readings
Onöhsagwë:de' Cultural Center, 75
ontological shock, 118–119
Oppenheim, Janet, 79

P

Parker, Charlie, 33
perception, altered, 121
performance and composition, simultaneous, 34
pets, connection with, 94, 103, 108
Pfahl, Jamie, 75
physical lineages, 107
physical mediumship, 95, 163. *See also* mediumship
places, connection with, 109–111
platform mediumship, 179
polyvagal theory, 50–53, 55, 97, 144
Porges, Stephen W., 50, 97, 144
possessions, 69
Post, Amy and Isaac, 80–81, 85
Powell, Diane Hennacy, 16
power, 72
precipitated paintings, 166–167
presence
  exploring within, 123–124
  mindfulness meditation practice and, 120–122
  practicing, 123–124, 144
  tethering and, 121–122
privacy. *See* confidentiality and privacy
professional associations, 44
professional mediumship. *See also* medium practitioners
  building safe and effective practice, 140–141
  cultural knowledge of, 134
  legal treatment of, 134–135
  noble suffering of, 138–139
  as sole proprietor, 137
  typical schedule for, 137–138
proprioception, 97, 100
psychic communication. *See* extrasensory perception (ESP)
psychic occurrences, unsolicited, 40
psychic services, in a capitalist framework, 134. *See also* professional mediumship

Q

Quakerism, 81
Quakers, 80
quantum theory, 17
quieting, 144–147

R

rapport, building, 37
reading checklist, 212
readings
  aftercare, 211
  as care work, 201
  category-led, 210
  checklist, 212
  closing, 211
  contact-led, 211
  content structure, 207
  defined, 38
  frequency of, 206
  as hard work, 202
  identifying the recipient of, 16
  location for, 204–205
  one-on-one, 201–202
  in-person or online, 204–205
  preamble, 207–208
  preparing for, 218
  scheduling, 203–204
  session time, 206
  shifting into mediumship during, 208–209
  sitters' role in, 205–6, 209–210, 211, 213–214
  starting the, 207
  structure of, 202–203
  support for sitter, 205
receptivity, 121
recordkeeping, 45
regulation, state of, 51, 121
relationships, 89, 93–94, 112–113. *See also* connection
resistance, 141
resource deficiency, 33
responsible mediumship. *See also* mediumship
  advice and, 44–45
  avoidance behaviors and, 42
  boundaries and, 65–68
  confidentiality and privacy, 43–44
  conscious-altering (*See* states of consciousness)
  delivery of service, 44
  delusion, potential for, 42
  discernment, 60–64
  ethics and (*See* ethics)
  fees and, 45

Index

informed consent and
  permission, 43
objectivity, 44–45
professional associations, 44
recordkeeping, 45
safe connections, 45–46
safety, 46–49
scope of practice, 44
supervision and, 44
unsolicited psychic
  occurrences and, 40–41
Ritchey, Shannon, 156
Rochester, Judith, 25, 163

S

safety
  external factors
    influencing, 144–145
  external pressures and, 53
  implicit, 53
  internal, 145
  of mediumship, 41–42
  neuroception and, 50
  promoting feelings of,
    144–145
  readiness and, 46–49
  tools for, 50
  uncomfortable vs unsafe, 49
Sapolsky, Robert M., 54
séances, 198–199
Seeman, Erik R., 83
segregation, 81
self, the, body and, 97
self-connection, 148
self-soothe space, 55
Seneca Nation, 75–76
senses, noticing the, 96–99
shadow self, 108
Sheldrake, Rupert, 16

simplified materialist model,
  24
social engagement, 51
social respectability, 84
somatic empathy, 96
soul senses, 25–26
soul/spiritual lineages,
  106–107
spirit realm/spirits
  connecting with, 70,
    180–181, 186
  guides, 109, 165
  identifying in a reading,
    181–184
spirit writing sessions, sample
  of, 7
Spiritualism. *See* Modern
  American Spiritualism
spiritualism
  creating a container, 65
  creativity and, 19
  data collection and, 24
  overview, 17–19, 79
spirituality, 83
spontaneity, 33
states of consciousness
  activities to shift, 47–48
  categories of, 46–47
  changing, 50–53
  co-regulation and, 56
  defensive, 50–51
  hypnagogic state, 47
  non-defensive, 51
  overview, 46–47
  shifting, 56–59
  social engagement, 51
  tools for changing, 55
substances, conscious-
  altering, 48

T

Taft, Ray, 75
tethering practices, 71,
  121–122
things, connection with,
  112–113
Thomas, Elaine, 190, 200
time travel, 131
trance mediumship, 22
transliving being, 19
transordinary mediumship,
  47–49, 117
transordinary state, 50–51
transphysical beings, 68
transphysical communication
  (TPC), 15–16, 220
transverbal data, 108
travel, attentional, 125–127

U

uncomfortable vs unsafe, 49
unknown dead, 104
unsafe space, 49
unseen world, belief in, 19
US Surgeon General,
  loneliness and isolation
  advisory, 88

V

vestibular system, 97
visionary art, 174–175

W

Wadsworth, Andrea, 41, 70,
  131
wholeness, accepting, 141
Windbridge Research Center,
  16
women's rights movement, 85

ACKNOWLEDGMENTS

This book is the progeny of so many connections through time and space. I wrote it because of my house, which drew me to this place and down this curious path, keeping me safe and cozy all along the way. I have this house because of the Pfahl family, whom I love so much for welcoming me as one of their own. The Pfahls have this house because of Lily Dale, which has welcomed many of its generations. I'm grateful to all my neighbors for making their lives here, and to all Lily Dale's residents, past and future. Lily Dale wouldn't exist without the Spiritualists, of whom I feel especially connected to and grateful for Amy Kirby Post, Maggie and Kate Fox, and Victoria Woodhull.

I wanted a team for this book, so it is by definition a dream team. My sister Hannah Pfahl is my constant support and best friend. Grace Kredell and Joanna Ebenstein believed in, helped, and encouraged me before and while I wrote it. I'm incredibly lucky to have an agent, Adrian Shirk, and an editor, Kate Zimmermann, who instantly understood me and my intentions for the book. They, and the folks at Union Square & Co., have been brilliant collaborators all along the way.

Charvonne Carlson, Kelly McCormick, Amanda Zackem, Gigi Semone, Maria de los Angeles Martens Serrano, and Heidi Light provided invaluable feedback for early drafts of the book, bringing a tiny bit of their immense wisdom and knowledge to the pages. Thank you to my teachers, classmates, peers, and clients who helped make me the medium, researcher, and writer I am. If it weren't for all the incredible people who took my Mediumship for Creativity classes through Morbid Anatomy, I wouldn't have been able to prototype the processes and explanations that fill these pages. A special thanks to my monthly development circle for giving me a place to experiment. Lots of love and appreciation to

Acknowledgments

the ever-growing community of practitioners, including those who filled out my survey, chatted informally, and shared their experiences.

I'm so grateful for my friends and family outside this peculiar little world, who support me no matter what I'm up to and who helped me keep my connection to the rest of life, with special thanks to my sisters Amara Pfahl, Brittney Dunlap, and Liz Alta Hayre.

I absolutely couldn't have written this book without Nika, Athena, Sylvester, and Coyo by my side. They were so ever-present that I wouldn't be surprised if they were in cahoots with the house to make it happen. I also relied heavily on my porch and sofa to support me while I wrote and water, Goodles, Wildgrain, CookUnity, and Sacred Grounds to properly hydrate, feed, and caffeinate me. I'm grateful to Jocelyn Bergan and Julia Cohen for helping to protect my time this year and easing me into the code-switching between this work and gov tech modernization. Bobby Lyte's Flow State playlists, along with Miles Davis and my forever muse, Brian Eno, were critical to getting words on pages. My number-one favorite way to soothe my nervous system during the last few months of writing was to watch *Star Trek: Voyager*. Thank you to the cast and crew for creating another world for me to visit.

I most definitely wouldn't have written this book if it weren't for all the spirits and contacts who have come through to me over the years. Thank you for showing me you are real, despite my persistent doubt. Without the hundreds of hours of walking in the Chautauqua County wilderness with Coyo, all those delightful smells and efficacious plants to inspire, my brain could never have let go enough to finish the book. If every ancestor all the way back hadn't lived their lives exactly as they did, especially my mom, Molly Harrison, and her mom, Joan Harrison, these pages would not exist. I am eternally grateful for every one of you.

Lastly, I am so happy I could be with myself enough to write this book. Thanks, Tiff. As I hand over my baby to the world, I send gratitude to everyone who picks her up with gentle curiosity and a genuine willingness to go beyond.

ABOUT THE AUTHOR

Tiffany Hopkins moved into her great-great grandmother's dilapidated cottage in Lily Dale, New York, the world's largest Spiritualist community, while starting an independent research and design firm in 2018. She has since worked with some of the world's largest companies, nonprofits, and government agencies, completely renovated the house, and, surprising herself as much as everyone else, became a medium. She started Normalize Talking to the Dead to create resources for the next generation of people who connect with the beyond. These include a podcast about mediumship and this, her first published book. Tiffany has degrees in cognitive science, interdisciplinary computing in the arts and music, and business. She loves living in a historic, forest-adjacent village but travels frequently for work, increased food options, and to see friends and family.